WOMAN'S GREATEST FRUSTRATION

NOT UNDERSTANDING HER HUSBAND

Adriana Calabria

A BOOK FOR WOMEN THAT EVERY MAN MUST READ

COMMENTS ABOUT
Woman's greatest frustration

The author, Adriana Calabria, focuses on the well-being of creation by counting on women, where men need them as wives and ideal helpers. The woman was planned by God from the beginning to receive love, care and protection from her husband. When loved, she will respond with respect, which is very good for the relationship between man and woman, as well as for the family.

The author captures, in this book, how God meets the needs of his beloved, talented and skilled daughters. Without a doubt, within these needs is the feeling of projection as a woman and mother, where she will be able to give love and receive love from her children and husband.

It is amazing how the crowning work of God's creation is detailed with women as the protagonist. She is in the mind of God and in future eternity as a participant in it. It is very praiseworthy to read how women are encouraged to have covenants with the Creator God and to trust Him, enjoying the responses to His promises.

It is inspiring to be able to learn from the covenant that God prepares in advance for man and woman, which I particularly call: an enterprise called family. In that area is where spouses manage to project themselves into a wonderful future, being able to be happy from a present organized by the Word of God.

Every woman needs greater security and stability. This book teaches that. I recommend it for this time.

I have three beautiful children, three beautiful grandchildren, daughter-in-law, son-in-law, and a thriving ministry with wonderful people.

My wife and I live a present in love; We work and strive every day to honor the Lord with our family, which began 33 years ago with a splendid, smiling and very happy woman, whom I love with all my heart, my mind and my strength.

I like to fall asleep holding her in my arms, waking up every morning to live another passionate day with her, and every detail, no matter how small, she can transform into big and special ones.

I present to you once again my beloved and beautiful wife, Dr. Adriana Calabria.

Dr. Osvaldo Díaz
Founder Apostle
Celebración Osvaldo Díaz Ministries (CODM)
North Carolina, USA

I positively believe that this book has all kinds of answers for every woman in her need. I am shocked to see how the Holy Spirit has guided the author to reach the heart of each woman to know the values and attributes with which God has designed her.

This wonderful book will be a great inspiration and guide for the woman of this time, the one who has lost her values, the marginalized, the mistreated, the abused, making her see how God has prophetically made her his ally in all of human creation.

Thank you, Dr. Adriana Calabria, for allowing yourself to be used as an instrument to bring hope to today's woman.

Prophet Dr. Mercedes Arias Feliciano
Y Llegó Jesús Ministry

Dr. Adriana Calabria, already in her first book, *Man's Greatest Frustration: not understanding his wife*, led us in a simple way to the universe of man, to understand reactions, emotions and feelings, and understand actions that derive from the lack of communication and a sick emotional intelligence, the result of the spiritual immaturity that is in many people.

Now in this second book, *Woman's Greatest Frustration: not understanding her husband*, Dr. Calabria also leads us through a labyrinth of situations in which we are going to learn in depth about women, about that woman with a divine purpose, about that great woman that God thought and designed before the creation of the world. That is why I dare to describe a little the woman that Dr. Calabria will talk about in this book, saying the following:
Being a woman implies that from the womb you are a winner and that you were chosen and marked with a purpose on this earth. Being a woman is sometimes carrying crosses and burdens that do not belong to us and have not allowed us to be, essentially, according to God's design.

To be a woman is to be a co-creator with our creator, therefore, a woman has a unique power on this earth: to carry in her womb the extension of the existence of the human race. We are fragile and strong; we are water and fire.

However, in this book, I discovered what the greatest frustration of both men and women is: not knowing how to communicate, not agreeing, not knowing how to combine the creative love of two different beings, but with necessary and vital energies for the "car" to work. Dr. Calabria will help you see, understand, pray and love those differences; because if "I am accelerated, and you don't understand me", and "I am a brake, and you don't understand me either", it is time to come closer and read this book that will lead you to know women in all their dimensions and thus do not continue frustrated (the man). And the woman, by rediscovering herself, will know who she really is, what her value is, her purpose in life, and, above all, she will meet the architect of her own story.

Jacqueline Tineo
Journalist- Integral Coach
Radio Producer
CEO of Pregón Latino Radio and Radio Amor FM
Founder President of De Mujer a Mujer Foundation

In my long editorial career, I had not known a direct and at the same time subtle writing style; brave and at the same time discreet; real and entertaining in describing everyday marital issues, yet facilitating immediate solutions. The kind of account that when you read, you smile, and immediately say: "That's the way it is."

Since Dr. Adriana Calabria tells us the marital days as they are and translates them into five languages, she creates great possibilities of helping couples see that, apart from the most complicated conflicts, life as a couple can become simple, happy, even fun and never monotonous. It is enough to learn to live it under some basic principles that she reveals.

Her first book breaks down the usual complaint that a man doesn't understand his wife. This second book shows the point of view of the woman who does not understand her husband. Among typical topics of men's behavior, the author presents the difficult and painful topic of abuse against women. She puts a stop to her usual conciliatory balance and is firm against this evil that affects society so much. She defines it with determination and opens two doors of alternatives. She does not need excess drama to expose her tenacious opposition, with restraint and firmness.

If you want to look into the true and simple realities of married life, and how to solve couples' problems, *Woman's Greatest Frustration: not understanding her husband* is the most practical and effective tool that should be in your home. I congratulate you, Dr. Adriana Calabria.

Pr. Ofelia Pérez, AWA
Published author
Spanish Editor, Whitaker House
Certified Author Consultant

I have always believed that the media is a great tool for spreading messages that transmit values, hope and new opportunities to our society.

My friend, Dr. Adriana Calabria, in her book: *Woman's Greatest Frustration: not understanding her husband*, which I consider a treasure, contains simple, practical and direct explanations and applications that will reach the hearts of thousands of marriages through the Word of God, and will bring hope, healing, restoration and liberation.

If you are a person who wants to achieve significant results, this book is for you. If you want to have a more productive life, this book is for you. If you think it is impossible for you to produce results and be useful in your marriage, this book is for you. If you are a leader or pastor, but want to help those who follow you be more productive, this book is for you.

Get ready, because what you will read next will change your life and lead you to grow. In your hands you have a powerful message from a great woman with a big heart.

Dr. Sandrie Serrano Bermudez, Apostle
Hands Global Pastors & Parachurch Min. Fellowship Network
New York/New Jersey

Unless otherwise indicated, all Scripture quotations have been taken from the The Holy Bible, English Standard Version® (ESV®) © 2001 by Crossway, a publishing ministry of Good News Publishers. All rights reserved. Scripture quotations marked (CEV) are from the Contemporary English Version Copyright © 1991, 1992, 1995 by American Bible Society. Used by Permission. Scripture quotations taken from the Amplified® Bible (AMP), Copyright © 2015 by The Lockman Foundation. Used by permission.

Edited by: Ofelia Pérez
OfeliaPerez.com

Woman's greatest frustration: Not understanding her husband
A book for women that every man must read

ISBN: 979-8-9899399 0-9

Printed in the United States of America
© 2023 by Adriana Calabria
Adriana Calabria Publishing, LLC

No part of this publication may be reproduced or transmitted in any way or by any electronic or mechanical means; including photocopying, recording or by any storage and retrieval system, without the prior written permission by the author.

DEDICATION

How can I not thank you, Holy Spirit, if every day you inspire me more and more to continue writing, using my light writer's hands to capture divine ideas that transform lives! Thank you, God, for bringing conviction, faith and wisdom that allow me to do what I love and am most passionate about: writing.

This book is dedicated to my husband, Apostle Osvaldo Díaz, whom I love and admire because he always comes out ahead in any circumstance. You are strong and brave.
And what can we say about Agustín, our first-born son, a man already so successful, like Domenico, our son-in-law, both with a wonderful future.

To our daughters, Damaris and Daniela, and Saraí, our daughter-in-law; They are beautiful.
Damaris is a complete woman; Daniela, so determined and with a firm character; and Saraí, so wise and intelligent, all three dedicated to the service of God.

It is a joy to have them in my life, they are a blessing. And my little ones Ethan, Liam and Arianna; How much happiness they bring every time they come to our house! I bless your lives.

RECOGNITIONS

Oh, my God, how many early mornings the Holy Spirit woke me up to give me the revelation of each chapter I wrote! I have lent you my hand, Jesus Christ and together we did it. Thank you, I am your ally.

I thank my husband who cared about giving me my time so I could have peace and tranquility to dedicate myself to writing. Every day he covers me with his love and makes me feel strong and safe. I'm lucky to have you.

To my mother, Ana María, thank you for taking such good care of me from the womb. I enjoy this time of maturity with you. You make me laugh, and I will always be your "baby."
I also dedicate this book to my aunt Julia. You are a young woman of 86 years and you will always be in my fond childhood memories. I appreciate our reunion, you have not changed, you are unique.

To my family, relatives, and acquaintances who showed their admiration when reading my first book and not only encouraged me to continue writing, but also eagerly asked me to finish this second book. Here it is.

To the pastors, ministers and spiritual family from different parts of the world who are part of the Kingdom of God, and with their faithfulness and love they have encouraged me. I appreciate you and you are very important to me.

To the intercessors, how wonderful to have you and rest in you who intercede twenty-four hours a day! May the Lord reward you abundantly.

To Pastor Maritza Mejía; How good that one day I convinced her to stay with me and not listen to the person who had brought her to church and wanted to separate her from the ways of God. You are a very valuable woman, predestined by God for this time and for *Celebración Osvaldo Díaz Ministries*.

And to my dear Ofelia Pérez, my favorite editor, I want to thank you because a couple of years ago you agreed to work not only on my first book, but also for having invested time in instructing and training me in the art of writing. Thank you for being sensitive to the voice of God and for having reunited us, oh how much I appreciate you. I declare the best over your life.

CONTENT

Prologue by Omayra Font		21
Introduction		23
1.	Women designed by God	29
2.	Your home: an extension of yourself	35
3.	No more patches; true transformation	41
4.	Flames in the heart	47
5.	Why don't you dress up a little more?	55
6.	The woman as a leader	59
7.	Your best friend, companion, and confidant	65
8.	A woman in love	73
9.	Call the accused	79
10.	Strong as steel, fragile as glass	83
11.	God becomes the sentinel of man and woman, for blessing or for judgment	85

12. The God of the mountains is also the God of the valleys	97
13. Love begins in the kitchen	101
14. Let yourself be formed by him	107
15. Guilty, who? I?	113
16. Complicated women	117
17. From love to hate	121
18. Before you get divorced… think twice	125
19. Fidelity is a virtue	129
20. He did it to me… I'll do it worse to him	137
21. I would like to fall in love with a great man	143
22. How to become a confident woman	151
23. I want to be rich	159
24. Never abandon your home	163
25. The man I chose	167
Epilogue: From my heart	173
Final words	175
About the author	177

PROLOGUE

I congratulate Dr. Adriana Calabria for her dedication to helping married couples understand each other beyond any particular and social characteristics that distinguish male and female character and behavior.

She describes daily married life in a way that is somewhere between real and funny, and that makes women and men read her messages and find solutions that sometimes get lost in the confusion of their respective contentions.

The woman who values herself, as I have emphasized in my books and the author of this book presents as a premise, correctly chooses her husband and her life partner, and gets to know him more and more.

She creates with him an invincible team in God, not only spiritual and ministerial, but also as parents and creators of a united and strong family, and of a marriage covenant that is strengthened, affirmed and grows over the years... where they overcome together the changes and adversities of life, and business creativity rises with a common goal.

The author writes: "woman is the crowning work of Creation, and when you understand this... you understand exactly the divine nature that lies within you... You have been chosen to mark a path to follow, from the beginning of eternity." These are great truths that, when we know them as daughters of God, there is no frustration in our marriage relationships because we were created by God to understand our husbands.

Know yourself, value yourself and transform yourself by reading this book. Say goodbye to frustration.

Omayra Font
Author of the *Woman* series
(Woman, value yourself; Woman, she dreams; Woman, create; Woman, build your own business; and Woman, celebrate)
Pastor of "Fuente de Agua Viva" Churches
Puerto Rico and Florida

INTRODUCTION

The first thing I want you to say with me is: "Thank you, Lord, for the blessing of being a woman! I am not a nanny! Not an employee! Not a maid!" I am a woman!". And being a woman is a special blessing.

There is so much to write about women... the ones who are always right, the ones that always say: "I told you so..." Right?

In short, the objective is to establish that as long as you do not know things about yourself that you did not imagine, you will not understand how to deal with the soul of man. Knowing your true nature will make you free and able to function in the different stages of your life. If you first manage to know yourself well, you will be able to understand in an extraordinary way the soul of man, his character, his customs, his reactions, and in that way, you will no longer live frustrated, bitter and not knowing what to do.

Precisely, frustration grows inside you and criticism towards the other person grows because you only see the defects. This produces continuous discomfort and dissatisfaction that accumulates day by day inside you.

I like a comment from preacher Kathryn Kuhlman, who was heavily criticized by some for being a woman in Christian ministry. She once said in her sermons: "No, I never think of myself as a woman preacher, I tell you the truth. I am a woman; I was born a woman and I try to maintain my place as a woman. Let me say something to women: Please, whatever you do, don't try to be a man! We were born women. I recognize the fact that I am a woman and I will try to be a lady. I never try to take the place or authority of a man. Never! I am a woman; I know my place and I know what God has called me to."

The first thing I want to establish in this book is that you need to become a woman who values herself, who knows how to love and respect herself, then, from this concept, we can delve into your soul and your spirit.

Once you value yourself, woman, you will feel so good that you will begin to dream, something you had already forgotten about: dreaming. Close your eyes, wherever you are, and dream. Nothing prevents you from dreaming, and seeing with your spiritual eyes what you want for yourself and those you love most. Because love is fundamental.

> *Jesus said unto him, Thou shalt love the Lord thy God with all thy heart, and with all thy soul, and with all thy mind. This is the first and great commandment. And the second is like unto it, Thou shalt love thy neighbour as thyself. (Matthew 22:37-39, KVJ).*

You can't love anyone if you don't love God, which will make you love yourself. Seeing in yourself all those virtues that God has placed in your life will be the determining factor in being able to love the work of God in yourself and in those around you.

Understand that when one is born again spiritually, it is natural to love other people, but I always say that whoever does not love himself, as this verse says, how can he love others?

INTRODUCTION

Make sure you're okay with yourself; This is a daily exercise that requires transparency and surviving natural circumstances, whether called ill-treatment, contempt, rejection or pain. Even in the midst of the moments where you are hurt the most, if you are sure of yourself, you will not feel desperate, you will wait for the storms of anger and arguments to pass, and you will make the best decisions for you and your future.

Because it is your faith that will lift you above your feelings, knowing that you must focus your attention on the One who loved you beyond your flaws, your reactions or your character: our Lord and Savior Jesus Christ. Let the strength of the Lord be manifested even in the midst of your weaknesses as his Word says. May the Holy Spirit make your countenance shine!

IT IS YOUR FAITH THAT WILL LIFT YOU ABOVE YOUR FEELINGS.

Be disciplined in your search for what God wants to speak to you through his Word, the Bible, source of all wisdom and wealth for our daily lives.

Never faint, even if you are tired, overwhelmed and worn out from suffering so much, because in God our entire being is renewed, our mind is filled with good thoughts, and there emerges the love that manifests itself, even if you do not understand how this happens.

I have verified that in moments of anguish the love of God is manifested in me, and I find in the Lord everything I need, that there is no person on earth who can give it to you. Then there his love makes me strong, as the song says, his eternity manifests itself in me and makes me see that whatever happens to me will last as long as I allow it to last.

Joy, woman, is not lost, it is given. It is given over to the enemy when you get angry with the person, without being able to see that the fight is against Satan himself, who will always try to destroy you, but he will not be able to do it. If you strengthen yourself in the Lord, you will find true life, the Zoe life, the abundant life that comes from Him.

Joyful, full of joy, happy

> *But my God shall supply all your need according to his riches in glory by Christ Jesus. (Phillipians 4:19, KJV).*

Those of us who are believing mothers always want to provide our children with everything they need. We feed them, clothe them, hug them, and keep them safe from everything, in addition to teaching them the Word of God. That is why our children can live a joyful life with a happy heart.

What if someone told you that God wants the same things for his daughters? The daughters that God wants to bless. Would you believe it? But it is true. God provides the best for us, his daughters, in every stage of life. He promises in His Word to supply everything we lack. Therefore, do not give up on your talents and abilities.
You must live joyful, full of joy and happy.

WOMEN DESIGNED BY GOD   1

> *"Since Genesis, the woman is the crowning work of Creation, and when you understand this, you acquire a value that does not give rise to frustration because you understand exactly the divine nature that lies within you."*

The first thing you have to understand is that you were in the mind of God before the foundation of the world. Extraordinary. You were in his mind and you were a divine idea, a predestined invention for a specific place and time.

That is why it is so important that you know your original design in detail, because that way you will be able to hold yourself firmly and without fainting during your walk in this life. It is very likely that you have not been effective until today in those areas where you are strong because you have not discovered your true potential. You make a difference even with thousands of mistakes made. You were formed for something very important and by knowing your design, you will understand that all these years God has been surrounding you because He wants you to get closer to Him. Have you ever thought about what our beloved God had in mind when he formed you?

If you think that you are nobody or that you are not worth enough, you will believe that everything that exists is for another woman, but not for you; that you have been forgotten.

> **HAVE YOU STOPPED TO THINK ABOUT WHAT GOD EXPECTS OF YOU?**

Have you stopped to think about what God expects of you?

God created us in eternity. God made you in eternity and when the time came you were implanted in your mother's womb. Some of us were kept firmly in that womb. My mother always told me that when she was pregnant with me, she had to rest because otherwise she ran the risk of losing me.

On one occasion she was prescribed a medicine that was to keep me and not abort me. My dad went to the pharmacy, bought the prescribed remedy, and upon returning home at the moment the nurse was going to give the injection, she realized that the medicine was abortive, that is, there was an error in the prescription. Can you imagine if God had not enlightened that nurse? I wouldn't be here alive. Without a doubt, my life was in the mind of the Lord. His plans were imprinted with eternity.

> *Who hath wrought and done it, calling the generations from the beginning? I the Lord, the first, and with the last; I am he. (Isaiah 41:4, KJV).*

You know why? Because we are also in the mind of God in future eternity because only He knows our end.

> *Your eyes saw my unformed substance; in your book were written, every one of them, the days that were formed for me, when as yet there was none of them. (Psalm 139:16, ESV).*

Nothing and no one can change the value that you have for God, but have you stopped to think that you do not value yourself enough? Of course, and by not valuing yourself you gradually lose your true identity. You look at other women and try to imitate them without understanding that you are unique and original, that God's grace has been poured out on you.

> *Your true identity now has the nature of God. According to the promise of 2 Peter 1:4, "we are partakers of the divine nature," that is, we acquire the true nature of God.*

To understand this principle, you must always please God because as a woman you will always want to please others, but when you experience true love, which is the love of God, you feel a security against anything.

The love of God is perfected in you and what you sow, you reap. Women were designed to receive love and to be protected. Every man should know this.

Since Genesis, the woman is the crowning work of Creation, and when you understand this, you acquire a value that does not give rise to frustration because you understand

SINCE GENESIS, THE WOMAN IS THE CROWNING WORK OF CREATION.

exactly the divine nature that lies within you.

You have been chosen to mark a path to follow, from the beginning of eternity. You should not think selfishly only of yourself; You have daughters who will follow your example because you are their model.

You do not want your descendants to go through the same thing that you have gone through. I like to say that when you accept new life in Christ, the blessings continue for a thousand generations after you.

> *Know therefore that the Lord your God is God, the faithful God who keeps covenant and steadfast love with those who love him and keep his commandments, to a thousand generations, (Deuteronomy 7:9, ESV).*

Everything you do in favor of knowing God more and advancing his Kingdom will bring blessing to your future generations. This is very powerful. Imagine what God offers us, His Love, and He is committed to remain in our descendants, because His Promises are yes and amen. I think it is worth following him, serving him and being faithful to him, right?

Your sons and daughters must follow the Christian life and to do so you have to be their example. Yes, you as a woman. Your family's well-being, prosperity and success depend on keeping covenants with God.

Covenants with God

Understand how the fact that God stops works. Think: He stops in the middle of the entire Universe to make covenants with us. This leads us to enter a deeper dimension with Him in our spiritual life.

It is the covenants that He makes with us that keep us firm in the calling. In my mind I always remember how the Lord, before calling us for full-time service, gave us such exact verses regarding what he would give us in the future, and today we have already seen the fulfillment of it.

What's more, I personally am very bold with God and I claim his promises, and what do you think He does? He answers me and fulfills them.

There will be times in your life that what will keep you firm in the ways of the Lord are His Promises. What gives us the power to be victorious in life are covenants with God because they allow an expansion of what God called us to do. So, are you willing to make covenants with God?

Spiritual life is not defined with words, but with obedience. The Word of God is absolute truth. His promises written there are for us his daughters, and all of them show us a powerful God making covenants with man and woman.

God has prepared a covenant for man and woman, so that when a man wants to have a sexual relationship with a woman, he does so through the marriage covenant and not outside of it, which is a sin. The enemy does the opposite: he incites people to live as they want, without law and without parameters, but this is something illicit. Living our lives in a covenant relationship with God will give us greater security and stability, and put us ahead of the future. And God will do so with those who are willing to do it. Think about it.

Since Genesis, the woman is the crowning work of Creation, and when you understand this, you acquire a value that does not give rise to frustration because you understand exactly the divine nature that lies within you.

YOUR HOME: AN EXTENSION OF YOURSELF

> *"Your home should be heaven itself, a place of peace, harmony, the center of our affections, and where our weaknesses are covered by the mantle of love."*

I have observed over the years that women repeat the stories of their mothers or grandmothers. They learn by observation. Everything you do in life is the result of experiences, of what you saw your elders do, and also of what they have taught you.

For this reason, life is so difficult for those women who have not had a role model, call it a mother, a woman, who teaches them everything that concerns a home. As well as, women who have had a mother, over the years do the same things that they did, good or bad. That's why when you do something wrong, your husband will always make you angry by saying, "You're just like your mother!"

In the world we live in, the reality is that we cannot confine women only to household chores, because there are great women who perform extraordinarily well in their different professions and are very useful and competent. However, in the midst of everything they do, we cannot help but say that the roles of mother and wife are irreplaceable.

From the time I was eighteen to thirty-eight, I had a judicial career, I worked for twenty years in the Federal Court in Argentina, and I was blessed that my husband always and unconditionally helped me with all the housework and childcare. That was very important to be able to progress, and for the good of our marriage. But I am aware that not all men are like him. What's more, I always admired his way of being, because I have heard complaints for years from so many women that they have to do everything alone because their husbands don't help them with anything, on the contrary, it is as if they had another child in their homes.

Praise and admiration

Something very fundamental comes in here. If you want your husband to play a helping role for you and your children in your home, you have to encourage him with words of praise every time he does something. The man is a very simple being, who is disarmed by the words of praise from his wife, and is very easily filled with anger if he is not understood.

> **STIMULATION THROUGH WORDS GENERATES A VERY POSITIVE ATTITUDE IN MAN**

That is why it is so important that you teach your children to admire him and reward him with positive attitudes towards their father; This way you will achieve anything from him. Stimulation through words generates a very positive attitude

YOUR HOME: AN EXTENSION OF YOURSELF

in man, in all aspects. The most important organ we have is the brain because it manages everything else in our body. If you send positive messages to the brain, the result will be positive attitudes.

If every day, the person who is with you highlights the best in you and not the mistakes, the result will be attitudes of service towards others.

Nothing makes a human being fall in love more than the other being attentive to him or her. In the case of marriage, the priority should not be the children, because they are "arrows" that we must launch into the world, says the Bible. [1]They are not ours, God lends them to us for a time, because when they grow up, they decide to create their own way. It is the law of life.

Your greatest focus should be on your husband, on that man with whom you fell in love, and with whom you must renew your passion day by day. It is said that marriage is like a garden; It requires a lot of love and a little work every day, and this is very true. The last thing you should neglect as a woman is your marriage.

One of the promises you both made was fidelity and mutual help on both sides. And the reality is that your mom or your grandmother taught you the opposite: you should only take great and exaggerated care of your children, and the poor man who contributed his part to have those heirs, you leave him abandoned, alone and lost.

---

[1] *Like arrows in the hand of a warrior are the children of one's youth. (Psalm 127:4)*

No, biblically, and according to Ephesians 5 (verses 25-28), God compares marriage to Jesus Christ and the Church. Imagine how high our Redeemer esteems marriage, for such an excellent comparison to exist.

Therefore, I want to teach you how to reprogram yourself mentally and spiritually so that you will be a successful woman and will be remembered as an excellent woman of God, but also as a complete person in all other areas of your existence.

For man, his work, what he does professionally or in his work performance, is his fulfillment. But for a woman, her home will always be. Her house, her garden, her area where she lives is her most important point of pride, and no matter how much the world advances, and fashions and magazines want to sell us something else, it will always be like this.

Many famous artists today appear in videos cooking, or showing their beautiful houses, one more beautiful than the other, and that happens because that environment reflects what you are, an extension of yourself. Your home is the most intimate and at the same time what has to do with your entire world. That is why it should be your headquarters of glory, your place of happiness, where you feel fulfilled, because it is your home.
It is the place where the center of our affections is located, where everyone who lives there must always want to return, where our friends and family want to come.

Our house is always being visited by our beautiful family. All of them visit us despite their many occupations, and the generations that come enjoy our meals, we laugh while we eat dinner, we chat animatedly and we spend indelible times in our minds and in those of the children.

They never forget their grandparents, or their aunts who make them play, and the delicious things they eat at our house. What do you think that creates in marriage? A great satisfaction of feeling fulfilled, and that things have been done very well, by the guidance of the Word of God.

> IT IS NEVER TOO LATE TO MODIFY WHAT WE HAVE LEARNED.

So, it is never too late to modify what we have learned, because according to the Apostle Peter, not everything we have learned from our parents hasbeen good and I am paraphrasing the verse, therefore, we must understand that there is a lot to learn. In our church, we have invested a lot of time, and we continue to do so, in teaching better living habits for homes.

The Word of God says that *"love covers all offenses" (Proverbs 10:12)*.
Your home should be heaven itself, a place of peace, harmony, the center of our affections, and where our weaknesses are covered by the mantle of love. Amen.

NO MORE PATCHES; TRUE TRANSFORMATION

3

"When you think you have done everything, I remind you that with God we have never done everything. He is always one step ahead of us."

There are times in life when we must stop and meditate on how we are moving forward. When God comes into our hearts, he operates very strong changes, and he needs true repentance from each of us.

He is not interested in amending your life, but in making very profound modifications, dramatic changes that will cost you the death of the self, and will achieve a true transformation in you.

There are those who use the word "restoration," and if we think about our old life, now in Christ we feel that we have been restored, that spiritual life has been returned to our soul, and that is so. But, since there are things that no longer serve you, God begins a transformation in you.

Transformation means that a metamorphosis occurs in you, a change of form, an internal reform that manifests itself on the outside. Everything that is crooked becomes straight. It is a regeneration, a new "genesis", a new beginning.

The way I see it, when something is restored, for example a car, they can fix the exterior cover, the seats, the tires, put an engine with more power, and it will remain right in front of you, "like new." But, underneath all those arrangements is an old car.

With God it is not like that, and there is an excellent verse that shows us the work of the Lord:

> *See, I have set you this day over nations and over kingdoms, to pluck up and to break down, to destroy and to overthrow, to build and to plant." (Jeremiah 1:10 ESV)*

There are women who experience very slight changes in their lives. If we compare them with women who do not have God, there are very few things that differentiate them from them. On the other hand, there are structured and legalistic women, who have strong holds in their minds due to their ignorance of the Word of God, not taking into account that each prohibition detailed in the Scriptures was for specific peoples or nations at a specific time... Others are aggressive, with a bad character, and speak unedifying language for her and those around her, especially her husband.

> **A WOMAN MUST HAVE CHARACTER AND CONDUCT. SHE HAS TO KNOW HOW TO SET HER OWN LIMITS.**

NO MORE PATCHES; TRUE TRANSFORMATION

A woman must have character and conduct. She has to know how to set her own limits, and let the Spirit of God do it. She should be sweet and kind with her words because every man is sensitive to a woman's words of praise; that is very powerful.

Therefore, God's proposal to destroy, ruin and tear down is precisely to be
able to build and plant everything new about Him in you.

Maybe you gave everything and received nothing and you said: enough! First there has to be a work that at first seems negative, painful, but that in the long run produces an "eternal weight of glory in you," as the Word says. Before a building task can be carried out, everything that is no longer useful must be removed. He will not make a minimal repair, in fact, God continues working in our lives until the end.

God blesses those who take this attitude, because above the advantages and comfort there is a woman who is willing to allow true transformation to occur. This will be reflected in her, because she will stop being frustrated, living a dull and unpredictable life, and without any plan for her destiny, but will understand how useful she is for the Kingdom of God and for the beings who love her.

Now, if we think about what it means to replant something, it is to lift from the roots a plant that already occupies the entire bottom of a pot, and move it to a larger one that will allow it to grow stronger, get bigger and be more fruitful. This makes the plant have more potential and capacity, so its roots will be deeper as well. How interesting! Right?

Therefore, how important it is to let God work in our lives!

> *He also told them a parable: "No one tears a piece from a new garment and puts it on an old garment. If he does, he will tear the new, and the piece from the new will not match the old. (Luke 5:36, ESV)*

This brings me to a conclusion. There comes a time when the dress is so worn out that the solution is better to throw away the old garment and save the new cloth to make another one. The thing is that today everyone wants to retain the comfort of this life or the methodology of the world, and not the treatment of God that in the long run produces lasting peace.

I love everything new, the smell of a new car, new and more advanced appliances, cellular devices, new clothes, everything that is advancement, validity. I like to live the life that God gave me. What's more, I always say: Live life! The path of this life is very long and the best way to travel it is with the strength that comes from God.

WITH GOD WE HAVE NEVER DONE EVERYTHING. HE IS ALWAYS ONE STEP AHEAD OF US.

Even when you think you have done everything, I remind you again that with God we have never done everything. He is always one step ahead of us.

Therefore, it is important that you understand that what you must achieve is the revelation of God's heart for your life, his new mercies every day; being understood of the times and the seasons we are living in; know his Word and put it into practice, act, help others achieve their goals and purposes.

Changes are difficult, since we cannot see the future and yet we are forced to let go of what we currently know, precisely so that the new can come.

Get ready, woman, to take action. There is something on God's agenda already prepared for you, your family or your ministry. No more patches, true transformation. transformation.

FLAMES IN THE HEART

4

"When a woman allows herself to be abused, she sets a precedent for her future generation."

I want to enter into this topic of abuse of women by first telling a testimony. I have three wonderful children, but since the two oldest are already married, we have our youngest daughter, Daniela, who is now 22 years old, living with us. All three were educated in a Christian institution and only knew school and church.

I really like talking to my daughter Daniela because she has the gift of discernment due to her Christian understanding, and when she speaks, she says things with great depth.
I was counseling a sister who said she was being treated very badly by her husband and I asked my daughter what her opinion was on the matter. Her response surprised me: "Once a woman allows a man to abuse her, she always will."

My daughter is so clear that a first time abuse should not be allowed, because if a woman allows herself to be abused just once, she will be abused for the rest of her life. In reality, when a woman allows herself to be abused, she forms a precedent for her future generation.

I felt proud of her because there is nothing better than the fact that a woman knows where the other's limits begin, and to have others respect hers. The limits are also with oneself; I must think and help others while still taking care of myself.

Regaining confidence in yourself will allow you to love more and hate less. If you invest time in that man who you feel is not for you, you will feed too much hatred. I always say that a woman endures, but when the moment comes when she becomes saturated, she makes decisions and does not turn back.

> YOU MUST KNOW HOW TO COME TOGETHER WHILE STILL BEING YOURSELF, WITHOUT SACRIFICING YOUR INDIVIDUALITY.

That's where you have to set limits quickly, before you get weary. Living your life being responsible for the feelings of others is not a life, much less if you have no control over your own feelings. You must know how to come together while still being yourself, without sacrificing your individuality.

Real man

Question: Is a true man an endangered species? Many years ago, the image of a man was a strong being, with a mustache, hair on his chest and a lot of authority; with codes of honor and morals, and responsibilities to fulfill in his role as head of the home; with a well-defined masculine identity and authentic maturity; someone who transmitted codes of life and experience to his descendants. Finally, and most importantly, man gave God a place of prominence in his heart.

Today we agree that it is very different, although the extremes are bad. Today man is an eternal adolescent; carried by any wind of fashion, he refuses to grow and mature. This is what is called an identity crisis: poor performance of roles established by God.

On the other hand, the "...I rule here and people say what I do..." does not help in any home. It is the authoritarianism that brings so much pain and wounds to family members from a sexist and despotic man. Without a doubt, something is failing in that being that God created to be the protector, supporter and caretaker of women and children. On the contrary, we see so much verbal and physical abuse that is poorly channeled dominance by men towards women.

There is a biblical concept that I want to rescue, said by Jesus Christ and that applies to a true man: ... *learn from me, for I am gentle and lowly in heart, and you will find rest for your souls (Matthew 11:29)*.

Being gentle or having gentleness does not mean that you are weak or without character, but it means power or controlled strength. It is the virtue of someone who governs his own spirit very well, and, therefore, his own life.

There is much greatness in a man who is gentle, as one of the characteristics of our beloved Savior, who displayed powerful wisdom emanating from his deep love for humanity. If the man manages to have control over his emotions, he will be someone in whom many

> **NOTHING MOVES GOD MORE THAN A HUMBLE MAN.**
>
>

will be able to see a gentleness accompanied by a power under control.

Nothing moves God more than a humble man, someone who comes to Him in the midst of his weaknesses and not his strengths. He says it in his Word:

> *But as for you, O man of God, flee these things. Pursue righteousness, godliness, faith, love, steadfastness, gentleness. (1 Timothy 6:11, ESV)*

Note that he is saying this to the man in particular, who must develop these qualities: to be calm, balanced, who can keep his passions under control, not reacting.

Someone I know could become gentle when his wife distanced from him and left him alone. You know that many men cannot be alone, much less sleep or eat alone. But in the midst of his loneliness God spoke to him, and he did so through many Bible verses.
The result was a total transformation, after years and years of constant struggles with his character and his way of being that not even he tolerated.

It is so important to accept changes, but how good it is to face changes while being sensitive to the voice of God.

> *Every good gift and every perfect gift is from above, coming down from the Father of lights, with whom there is no variation or shadow due to change. (James 1:17, ESV)*

God's will is good, says his Word. There is no situation, there is no problem that He cannot transform, nor wall that you cannot overcome with God's help. So whenever one seeks help, someone will be there to lend a hand. You do not need to endure any type of emotional or physical abuse. The Bible says to man: *Husbands, love your wives, and do not be harsh with them. (Colossians 3:19, ESV)*

> *Likewise, husbands, live with your wives in an understanding way, showing honor to the woman as the weaker vessel, since they are heirs with you of the grace of life, so that your prayers may not be hindered.*
> *(1 Peter 3:7, ESV)*

I want to help you, woman, to make some changes first in yourself, which I assure you, will modify all forms of aggression and contempt. The woman must be treated delicately. Do not open a spiritual door for your offspring, daughter of an abuser and married to an abuser. What do you think your children will learn? To be abusers. Something's not logical, right? Your children cannot continue with that cycle. Man's mistreatment of women is poorly channeled dominion and it is diabolical.

The cycle of generational curses

When we come to Christ, we must be free from generational curses. It is very important to know your family tree because many know about their parents or grandparents, but not about their great-grandparents, so we live in ignorance without taking into account inheritance.

Heredity is not just the color of eyes or skin, but the patterns of behavior that are repeated from generation to generation. If the grandmother had this or that illness, her mother and her daughter have it again, that is, the curses and also the sins are transferred, continuing in a vicious circle.

Those curses say the Scriptures reach up to the third and fourth generation.

> *You shall not bow down to them or serve them; for I the Lord your God am a jealous God, visiting the iniquity of the fathers on the children to the third and fourth generation... (Deuteronomy 5:9, ESV)*

But when God renews his covenant with Israel, he promises to bless the next thousand generations, that is, starting with each one of us, the following generations are blessed.

> *maintaining faithful love to a thousand generations, forgiving iniquity, rebellion, and sin. But he will not leave the guilty unpunished, bringing the consequences of the fathers' iniquity on the children and grandchildren to the third and fourth generation. (Exodus 34:7, CSB)*

I like to say that my life is from the cross onwards, that is, the sacrifice of Jesus Christ frees me from all those generational curses, because He paid the price for all our sins to break that disastrous cycle.

In my sermons, I always say that women can have a painless birth. It happened to me with my three children. I have not suffered anything, in fact, I arrived at the delivery room and on time they were born, but previously during the nine months I decreed that this was going to happen.

Furthermore, confessing the Word of God out loud will drive the enemy back; talking about the goodness of God and how his great love is upon our lives, makes us act offensively against the evil plans of the devil.

> **IF YOU WANT TO PLEASE THE LORD, YOU CANNOT TOLERATE ABUSE.**

If you want to please the Lord, you cannot tolerate abuse. You need to be sure that you are pleasing Him with your actions. If you don't, you will have unrealistic expectations that will lead to your own failure, because there will always be a man who frustrates you because no one changes anyone. If you thought you could change him, that's not the case. Only God transforms people.

Finally, you must act with wisdom and seek with all your heart, with all your soul and with all your mind the help that comes from above, and that in God you can have a refuge to turn to.

> *The Lord is a stronghold for the oppressed, a stronghold in times of trouble. And those who know your name put their trust in you, for you, O Lord, have not forsaken those who seek you. (Psalm 9:9-10, ESV)*

Depending on the attitude you take, your life will be a life of misfortune and misery or a life of blessing and joy. Every time you allow yourself to be abused, your quality of life is reduced.

Before entering our eternity with Jesus Christ, this is the only life we have and we must honor it, because it is a privilege that the Lord grants us minute by minute.
So come on, free yourself, and enter your new dimension holding the hand of Jesus Christ because He tells you: *I help you... (Isaiah 41:13)*

No two days are the same and with the arrival of each dawn come new opportunities to make a decision and always keep your life in constant discipline.

WHY DON'T YOU DRESS UP A LITTLE MORE? 5

> *"When you always look beautiful it produces in the man thousands of thoughts and fantasies that make him think of you the rest of the day."*

Most men like their wife to take care of their image, moreover, they enjoy seeing her well fixed, wear makeup without any special occasion, but do it only for him. This produces thousands of thoughts and fantasies in the man that make him think of you the rest of the day.

It is very important that she is aware of her natural beauty and highlight her attributes, always for him to see her and praise her. But some women are very vain, and dress up so that all men see her, not just her husband.

The man enjoys seeing his wife well dressed. We do not speak in the sense that the woman is presumed, or that for her to look pretty is a prevailing need. Rather, it is about the woman being aware of how beautiful her nature is and for her to worry about highlighting her attributes from time to time, not calling attention in a vulgar way, because it is very important for the man that his wife is put together and looks good.

What do you achieve with this? Passion, even with the passage of time. While love is constantly tested, one of the factors that weakens it is routine and physical carelessness. It is proven. Innumerable couples have separated because a more beautiful and physically attractive woman conquered the heart and mind of man. Remember, to man everything enters through their eyes.

And today the world is at war on fidelity and marriage, seeking to redefine something that God already established: purity, holiness and mutual love.

When your soul is caressed with beautiful words caused by your beauty, will produce something very powerful within you. Of course, this will require a small effort from yours, highlight your virtues alone and only for that man you love. But firstly, for you.

CHEERING UP AND LIVING HAPPILY WILL BRING WELL-BEING TO YOUR SURROUNDINGS AND YOURSELF.

For example, every day that I wake up I clean the skin of my face very well, and I also take care of my body with exfoliation and creams so that it is soft to the touch. I also do my makeup because I personally like to look good for myself, and as I go about my day, I like to look in the mirror. I don't feel it as an obligation, but as something natural, intrinsic in my person. Of course, depending on the way I fix my eyes or my lips, then

I see other women who imitate me in the way of doing my makeup. And my husband is my eternal crush.

That is why religiosity frustrated the life of so many beautiful women who do not know how to combine their spiritual life with their physical life. Taking care of your health, eating healthy, exercising, thermal baths and caring for your skin requires time and money, which is not always available.

But look in the mirror and remember this verse: *A glad heart makes a cheerful face ... (Proverbs 15:13).*

Having a reasonable mind suits your health. However, being envious destroys you to the depths of your being. Cheering up and living happily will bring well-being to your surroundings and yourself. Be objective with yourself and understand that there are things that you will not be able to modify, but there are other things that you can.

It is good for you to help him, year after year, to be better, to tell him in the best way how you want to see him. What clothes you want him to wear, if you want him to get on diet and exercise and, of course, you together with him.

While fidelity and intimate relationships in the couple are fundamental, cooking together encourages unity on the affective

> WHILE FIDELITY AND INTIMATE RELATIONSHIPS IN THE COUPLE ARE FUNDAMENTAL, COOKING TOGETHER ENCOURAGES UNITY ON THE AFFECTIVE BOND.

bond. It powerfully reinforces the feelings of well-being, because it is something fun, very relaxing and enhances love, because your bodies collide or your hands intersect while making a meal together. If you also prepare a romantic dinner, it will be love for two, which will become more than a day. It will be a very special moment that will renew you, making you complicit in something and you will be able to talk, make plans and exchange ideas.

In my case, when my husband cooks with me he helps me take a weight off because he does it faster than me, and he has an excellent way of giving the food a special flavor. Do not scold him if something is wrong. Be patient and remember that you can teach him and, on another occasion, he will be of great help when you need it, even if he asks you a thousand times how to turn on the oven.

On the other hand, cooking is a time when you are alone, much more productive than going to a restaurant because you are at home, in intimacy and can interact in many ways. And keep this in mind: everything you do together produces excellent durable results.

THE WOMAN AS A LEADER 6

"Leadership is something women are born with, even if any man wants to stop you, you are good in what you do. Always something in you will make you stand out".

The woman is a leader by nature. She is a leader in her home, with her children, in her work, and this has nothing to do with authority. For example, if you make a coffee, no one else will do it better than you, so you are a specialist in that.

I remember the time that worked in the Judicial Branch, we were a nice group of co-workers in the office, and when break time came, we would share some snacks and sweets, and it was always I that had to make the coffee. As much as I taught other co-workers how to do so it was not the same, they said, and I ended up doing it every day, "because it tasted different".

This is the case to this day with so many other meals that I make. What do I want to teach you with this example? That everything in which you are predominant, you are a leader.

It is something women are born with. even if any man wants to stop you, you are good in what you do. Always something in you will make you stand out.

> **KINDNESS OPENS SO MANY DOORS AND MAKES THOSE WHO KNOW YOU HAPPY.**

Kindness opens so many doors and makes those who know you happy. I remember there was a time when we had several concerts in our church, and there were opportunities in which some Christian singers came to dinner at our house. In one of the many dinners, being my husband and my children there also, a sister who was part of the leadership asked the guest singer who was sitting at our table if he wanted ice cream, to which he replied that he did not and thanked her.

We continued talking, about half an hour passed and I personally offered him ice cream again, to which he replied yes. Then, everyone turned to look at him, and laughed, but the singer added: "it was the way she offered it to me." I never forget this incident, because when you are kind, people accept you and value you, and it is always the favor of God operating in your life, which inspires and allows others to accept what you want to give.

That is true leadership; being able to excel at something and do it as a service to others, being useful and effective in what you have a predominant gift for.

To do this you must know yourself very well, and seek to develop more strongly what you are strong at and have good self-esteem, a high concept of your talents, which you will use for the benefit of others, but which will return to you as a boomerang.

You sow love, you will receive love. You call others, they will call you.

Extraordinary. Because the Bible says: ... *whatever you wish that others would do to you, do also to them... (Matthew 7:12, ESV).*

Look at this beautiful Word of God: *God, the Lord, is my strength; he makes my feet like the deer's; he makes me tread on my high places. (Habakkuk 3:19, ESV).*

Therefore, your path must always be upward, having a continuous banquet of joy, because you will be a model, other women who need a good example and a joyful spirit will follow you and adhere to you. You must live life intensely, in such a way that it is worth waking up every day, because you know that you have a very transcendent and important role to play. And you will have the favor of God and also of men, without them attacking you or considering you an object or someone inferior.

All the time I see women emerge so useful for the service of God, who have a beautiful heart, tremendous potential, but who have not been valued or appreciated. But, woman, once again, it is time to start with you, give yourself the opportunity to be different, to love yourself because every woman has a particular and special beauty.

IT IS TIME TO START WITH YOU, GIVE YOURSELF THE OPPORTUNITY TO BE DIFFERENT.

That's why you should ask yourself: What is my motivation in life?

> *For it is God who works in you, both to will and to work for his good pleasure.*
> *(Philippians 2:13, ESV)*

Furthermore, everything that comes from the heart of God is good.
This principle is that if what motivates you is to perform good actions in favor of others, without a doubt, you will be obeying the precepts of the Lord.
God wants it that way. The effect that salvation produces on a person's life is evidence of the good fruits in your life.

Always think about what your motivation is and why you do what you do.

I believe that transformed women are needed to raise their voices in this time, teaching the truth of the Word of God, and in this you must become an expert.
I always teach that there is a biblical ministry for women who are in subjection, under authority and coverage. The Bible says it:

> *There is neither Jew nor Greek, there is neither slave[a] nor free, there is no male and female, for you are all one in Christ Jesus.*
> *(Galatians 3:28, ESV)*

Some men lost focus on their design and women are God's answer today, otherwise think how many souls would be lost. I see year after year how women are standing out more and more in areas that were occupied by men, including social networks, and they do it so well that they are worthy of admiration.

> *He answered, "I tell you, if these were*

> *silent, the very stones would cry out." (Luke 19:40, ESV)*

It is impossible not to talk about the miracles, signs and wonders that our beloved Savior Jesus Christ has done for us, right? Think that women brought the Word of God by the Holy Spirit, and even prophesied what was accepted in the early church.

> *On the next day we departed and came to Caesarea, and we entered the house of Philip the evangelist, who was one of the seven, and stayed with him. He had four unmarried daughters, who prophesied. (Acts 21:8-9, ESV).*

Women also occupied a place in the Upper Room, waiting for the coming of the Holy Spirit and the beginning of the Church.

He goes before you opening doors that you could never open on your own.
You are very important to God; I like to say that God thinks of you. All the goodness of heaven was poured out when He created you.

*All the goodness
of heaven was
poured out when
He created you.*

YOUR BEST FRIEND, COMPANION, AND CONFIDANT

7

> *"If, as time goes by, your husband still includes you in his plans, because he understands that he is stronger and safer if he has you, and he cares about what you think, it is because you have someone at your side who values you and loves you".*

Oh, how you wish with all your heart that this man who is so difficult for you to understand, be your best friend, your companion and also your confidant! That requires a lot of your time invested in that man, and that you learn to fully trust him.

That is why it is so important to start with yourself. Look what this verse says:

> *Be beautiful in your heart by being gentle and quiet. This kind of beauty will last, and God considers it very special. (1 Peter 3:4, CEV)*

WOMAN'S GREATEST **FRUSTRATION**

Quiet…but how.

To deal with a man you need a lot of stability, a lot of self-confidence and a lot of patience. You also need to understand that he needs to know that he is your hero, that he always has a princess to rescue.

> **YOU HAVE TO ALWAYS HAVE IDEAS, IDEAS AND MORE IDEAS TO PUSH HIM TO ACHIEVE INCREASINGLY CHALLENGING GOALS.**
>
>

Life is too boring for him if you also want to settle him in the security of a very warm and toasty home, with delicious food and a bed to rest. He needs something more. He needs motivation in everything he does. You have to always have ideas, ideas and more ideas to push him to achieve increasingly challenging goals, whether in his job competing for a higher position, or in serving God in the area where his pastor has placed him; sometimes granting his wish to buy the latest model car (remember how many things he gifts you that you like) or going on that safari where he can be in contact with the animals.

I remember when I went with my husband to the Kruger National Park in South Africa, on a safari. We were going with our children and another couple, and my husband was so enthusiastic about getting to the place (he had already gone the year before) that he drove quickly through the mountains and I, who know him, realized his desire to show me, mainly me, the place.

What do you think I did when I saw the first giraffe? I let out a scream that I think made everyone in the truck startle. I was excited and celebrated having been the first to discover those animals in the middle of the jungle.

My husband, how happy he was when I continued praising the elephants, the lions. It was all a fun adventure for him and me, as well as for the other members. If I love going to the beach, but he likes going to the jungle, I have to be willing and give room to his tastes too.
Women are sometimes very selfish. We only look out for ourselves and forget about that precious man that God gave us, and who is also fragile, because if not, the Bible would not say that the woman is the... *weaker vessel*... (1 Peter 3:7).

You cannot ignore his authority, because God already established it that way; you must respect it. There is nothing more powerful than a woman who respects her husband. You cannot ignore this, nor believe that you will be on a lower level, because you will be doing it for love.
Then, he will make you feel loved, cared for and protected because there is no man who can resist the kind words of a woman.

Woman, you are special, you were formed by God for greatness, for the transcendent, to make that man your friend, your confidant. Like when you fell in love with him...
God does not miss anything. Psalm 103:14 says that...He knows our condition; he remembers that we are dust. In other words, God knew what the behavior of human beings would be.

> WOMAN, YOU ARE SPECIAL, YOU WERE FORMED BY GOD FOR GREATNESS, FOR THE TRANSCENDENT.

If we look at chapters 1 and 2 of the book of Genesis, they are extraordinary, because it is God fused with man in a complete communion. There was no sin, therefore, there was no illness, no pain, no depression.

> *And God saw everything that he had made, and behold, it was very good. (Genesis 1:31, ESV).*

Everything He had created was perfect for human beings to enjoy. But from chapter 3 of the book of Genesis until the end of Revelation, it is God speaking to human beings to restore them and return them to their original state. This is why we will see the restoration of all things starting with the Second Coming of our Lord Jesus Christ. Plus, He loves knowing that you want to be with Him more than anyone else on earth.

A true story

I am a fan of a very talented Spanish singer whose husband was a very famous bullfighter, and when they got married, it was the wedding of the year. She, in all the photos together with her husband, has an expression of love and admiration so deep that its touching, and in all the reports she expresses it with beautiful statements towards him.

After a year and seven months of marriage, he tragically dies from being gored by a bull and she becomes "the widow of Spain." For thirty years until today that is what she is called.

The interesting thing about this story is that, despite the years that have passed, she speaks of her husband as someone extraordinary. She continues to honor him with

YOUR BEST FRIEND, COMPANION, AND CONFIDANT

her words, she mentions him in her reports and continues to dedicate songs to him.

I tell this story because I find it so interesting that, although time passes, this famous woman has a vivid memory of a man who she spent very few years of her life with, but who marked her forever. He was her friend, companion and confidant.

This is how you should do; elevate that man in your life by feeling that he is the most extraordinary being on earth, because he is your friend, companion and confidant. That will make the years go by and your husband will be your friend. This must be worked on a basis of total trust. Yes, friendship is forged in a marriage.

It is so nice to remember the moments before the courtship, the first days of marriage, and the adventures lived together... the first kiss, the way you walked hand in hand together, the anxiety to see each other and talk to each other on the phone in the afternoons after work.

I always tell those who know me that my husband is my boyfriend, because he never stops courting me,

> IF, AS TIME GOES BY, YOUR HUSBAND STILL INCLUDES YOU IN HIS PLANS, BECAUSE HE UNDERSTANDS THAT HE IS STRONGER AND SAFER IF HE HAS YOU, AND HE CARES ABOUT WHAT YOU THINK, IT IS BECAUSE YOU HAVE SOMEONE AT YOUR SIDE WHO VALUES YOU AND LOVES YOU.

and because we continue to have as much fun together as when we were young. But he is also my friend, since we are both people who, due to our calling to the Christian ministry, spend all day together, however, this never caused us any inconvenience because we enjoy each other's company.

If, as time goes by, your husband still includes you in his plans, because he understands that he is stronger and safer if he has you, and he cares about what you think, it is because you have someone at your side who values you and loves you.

An example not to imitate

I met a young couple who bought their first house with a lot of sacrifice, and in one year they finished paying it off. Because he was a person who liked to do business, he talked to her about mortgaging her house and thus obtaining money to enter a sales circle that seemed very promising.

She refuses to sign a mortgage on the house because she understands that it is a very necessary asset and on top of that a third person would be in charge of making the payments, which causes distrust.

It is always said that women have a sixth sense, and she did not feel peace or security about signing the mortgage. He insists. Here comes something that I want to explain that many times women give in to men, and that is that in order to satisfy him and avoid arguments, they agree to do something that, if they said no at the moment, they would avoid a lot of trouble.

What was the ending to this story? The person who was

supposed to pay the mortgage did not do so and this young couple lost their house.

This experience served him well for the rest of his life because he promised his wife not to do anything again without her consent and that when he asked her about something, and she expressed her point of view, he would take it into account.

I have seen throughout my life so many men make decisions without considering the opinion of their wives and then suffer so many evils, without also taking into account the rules established in the Word of God, which, if you know them, will give you the wisdom necessary for everything you do.

All the promises of God established in the Bible are to be fulfilled and not to be transgressed, because *"whatever a man sows, that he will also reap…"*

Therefore, every man must recognize his mistakes and not be ashamed to ask forgiveness for his failures, leaving aside his pride; help her fulfill her dreams, her wishes and her deepest desires; and pay attention to his wife, pay attention to the details, and surprise her all the time.

He will always need to have access to you, I reiterate, he being your priority, woman, accepting those moments where he hugs you or kisses you without you asking him because it is spontaneous and it brings you out of your sadness and silence.

Laughter is an expression of joy. Just think how many times a day you smile and have fun with him. You can give yourself permission and laugh from time to time. Even when problems come, laugh, and the problems will not hurt you because they will find you with a happy spirit, which will make the matter more bearable.

The Word of God in Job 5:21-22, CEV says:

> *You will be sheltered, without fear of hurtful words or any other weapon. You will laugh at the threat of destruction and famine. And you won't be afraid of wild animals.*

This is resting in the protection of the Lord, against all odds and circumstances. Extraordinary and powerful.

A WOMAN IN LOVE   8

> "A man always falls for the charms of a woman in love, especially if she smiles. Even if he hasn't told you, after the first impression of your beauty, there is no man who can resist a woman who smiles."

Men who have a beautiful woman by their side change their perception of other women. Although others present to him as a Miss Universe.

All his strength as a man and his opinions are dismantled in the face of a well-dressed, charming and beautiful woman.

That is the power that God gave to women. Beauty.

And beauty is achieved, it is worked for, it requires time and a bit of effort on your part, but it brings great rewards in the long term.

The man always falls under the charms of a woman in love.

THERE IS NO MAN WHO CAN RESIST A WOMAN WHO SMILES.

Especially if she smiles. Even if he hasn't told you, after the first impression of your beauty, there is no man who can resist a woman who smiles.

If we think of a baby, the first thing he sees is the face of his mother who speaks to him smiling and it is certainly impossible for his mother not to be able to make him smile. The baby always smiles with his mother, so it is natural that when he grows up, he will be attracted to a woman who smiles.

If he likes you and you smile at him, it is an indescribable feeling for him. When I am serious or thoughtful, my husband says to me: "Are you okay?" Because I'm usually smiling, or listening to music, or singing, or dancing. In other words, I always aim to smile and be happy, it's my decision.

A woman in love shows off her husband or her boyfriend to other people. It's good because you raise his self-esteem and show your admiration for him. Posting a photo together and writing about how he loves you and your relationship with him over the years is wonderful and productive.

Another characteristic that you should highlight in yourself is to become an expert in all matters of life. Sometimes I laugh at myself because I get asked about everything. That is because I am allowing the work of God in my person to be real, through his Word and his Holy Spirit, but also because I read, research and educate myself always, being able to talk about any topic.

This is essential, because there will be days where you will be the one carrying the thread of a conversation, and you will put a topic on the table to have an interesting talk together.

The quarrelsome woman

What to say about the woman with the continuous complaint? The Bible talks about the quarrelsome woman. She is the one who causes discord, fights and upsets. She is always in a bad mood and explodes at anything. "Anyway, let everyone else put up with me... today I feel like this..." she usually says, without measuring the consequences. This is not a characteristic of a woman in love, quite the opposite, but I cannot help but mention it because there is a passage in Scripture that exposes this woman.

> *It is better to live in a corner of the housetop than in a house shared with a quarrelsome wife. (Proverbs 21:9, ESV).*

She is so unbearable that her chronic bad mood infects her entire family. Sometimes, the woman tends to use manipulation in all its forms to get something in return, so that the man does what she wants in her way, and then she ends up being a slave to her actions.

What this Bible verse means is that when there is such a woman in a house, the members of the family prefer to be anywhere but at home. She is the one who, when you say "Good morning," gives you a withering look and wants to tell you: "It will be a good morning for you... what is so good about this day...?"

She is the one who very rarely gives in to an argument and never admits that she is wrong. Simply put, a quarrelsome woman can drive you crazy.

Look, analyze yourself, because it's not always the others' fault and learn to apologize, even if you're not completely right. Asking for forgiveness is not lowering yourself, it is allowing your heart to remain healthy. It is letting go of those people that you have imprisoned in your life.

I have spoken with many daughters hurt by mothers like

this, who repeat the same story later with their children. They are angry and quarrelsome. When you see a dull man, without strength and without vigor, that is what these women have done to them. This does not represent a woman in love.

It is necessary for her to have true communion with God because it will be her only source of change in her life; it requires an internal healing of the heart, a real liberation from this curse that accompanies her throughout her life. It is not the Lord's will for you to live bitter and angry, because this is the fruit of hatred and resentment, which is contrary to the nature of Christ.

Leave the fight now. Jesus Christ is the Prince of Peace, and we are called to live in peace and in love, the best state for women.

Ruined and predictable women don't conquer anyone. You have to be spontaneous, witty. Take initiative…invite him out to a restaurant. A man loves a determined woman who already has plans made.

I usually do this with my husband, and I don't wait for a special date. One or two days a week we set aside for ourselves, just the two of us. It is a special time where we talk, we laugh, and I always ask him a special question, such as, for example: "Tell me what vision you have of your future…". Then my beloved husband, who is thinking all the time, begins to tell me: "I have this plan for our ministry, this plan for our family, this arrangement or modification for our house…"

The vision you have of your future injects adrenaline into your present.

We are never bored, and look, we spend twenty-four hours a day together! But we have never lost the love and passion for our marriage. We don't allow routine to kill our love. That's why, after so many years, I can say that I am more in love than the first day we met. Because love is like a garden, you must cultivate it and take care of it. Otherwise, it dries up and dies.

Happiness is like a magnet; it attracts. If you are individually happy, you will spread it to everyone around you.

> **THE VISION YOU HAVE OF YOUR FUTURE INJECTS ADRENALINE INTO YOUR PRESENT.**

Research at the United States National Institute of Health concluded that a happy woman causes excitement in men, making them see her as more attractive. A woman's smile can generate profound changes in the male gender.

So, you have to resolve to be happy. This is your determination and no one but you can do it.

If you gave too much...

It seems to be a characteristic of many women to love their partner or her husband so much, to the point of being empty and exhausted because they gave everything. You're tired of crying, of feeling ignored, you're tired of waiting for a change from that man who thinks he's indispensable. Then that's where you give up.

But I want to teach you something powerful. At this time in your life is when you have to cultivate yourself. Seek God with all your strength and allow the Holy Spirit to minister to your entire inner being. Swim in the waters of divine healing, because there is no better path than the real and true search for your spiritual life, because only God fills that inner void. It is in your spirit that He does the work and from there He heals your entire being.

Then, the true transformation begins, from within you, and from there you are a new and restored woman. Since God is a God of opportunities, pray for a man to come into your life who will love you and make you fall in love. You have not been called to suffer, God calls us to live in peace, remember: our beloved Savior Jesus Christ is the Prince of Peace. You are not alone; God is with you and you have every right to be a woman in love.

CALL THE ACCUSED 9

"You have the right to remain silent. Anything you say can and will be used against you in a court of law."

We have heard this phrase many times in numerous movies or television series about detention cases and legal trials, with lawyers and judges.
Most situations experienced between a man and a woman where there is a conflict, sometimes both come out harmed. One of the characteristics of women is to become judges of men.

When a person is detained, at the time of the arrest he must be informed of the reason why his freedom was prevented, and without wasting time the accusation against him is read to him.

The woman takes the position of judge because she does not agree on those actions that the man performs. It is also true that she believes that she can do better than him. But you must have balance because no one wants to live with oppression, or with a dagger stuck in their back.

There is a biblical story about Jacob that I find very consistent with what I am telling you. Jacob wrestled all night with an angel of the Lord and the result was that he was left with a limp when he walked. He came out of that experience with two things: he achieved God's blessing, but the limp accompanied him for the rest of his life.

The limp was a mark on his body of having gone through a painful experience and still achieving what he wanted, for God to bless him.

One of the enemy's traps is deception, but, although Jacob was a deceiver, the Bible says that he had... *seen God face to face, and yet his life had been delivered (Genesis 32:30).*

Although in this story it seems that Jacob was harmed by his limp in his hip, he achieved something more than that: his soul was saved. It is precisely with the soul that we relate to people and have conscience, which is what allows us to have knowledge of good and evil to carry out all our actions.

> **ASK GOD TO SEND THE SPIRIT OF TRUTH SO THAT ALL THINGS AND SITUATIONS BECOME CLEAR.**

Since words are like daggers, it is very difficult for a man to dodge a woman's verbal insults and shots. Maybe he didn't do what you think he did. In some cases, these are pure lies. ThVerefore, ask God to enlarge your heart so that you have the ability to forgive and not judge, to apply mercy instead of judgment, and that the evil that others have sent against you, God will use for good. Ask God to send the Spirit of Truth so that all things and situations become clear.

There is a throne of mercy, according to the Word of God, *where we can with confidence draw near to the throne of grace, that we may receive mercy and find grace to help in time of need. (Hebrews 4:16)*. In this way you will be putting into practice the biblical principles that will give you success in everything you undertake.

STRONG AS STEEL, FRAGILE AS GLASS

10

Strength and dignity are her clothing, and she laughs at the time to come. (Proverbs 31:25)

How can a woman be strong as steel and fragile as glass? She is a powerful spiritual warrior in the middle of the battle, solving thousands of problems and moving forward, but she, she is the one who is only allowed to show herself fragile and cry in the presence of God.

This is who she is and she positions herself: a tremendous and powerful woman of God.
She is knowledge combined with wisdom, intelligence applied at the right time, she is blessed in everything she does. She dresses in strength and honor, she laughs at what is to come, she provides for her children and her family, she is not afraid of anything.

SHE ALWAYS REMAINS STANDING IN EVERY CIRCUMSTANCE IN HER LIFE.

She does everything possible to make her finances work. She prepares for the future.

She always remains standing in every circumstance in her life. She believes God with all her heart and trusts that Jesus Christ promised her that He would be with her until the end of the world.

She carries a smile on her face and many secrets in her heart, because only she understands what she has been through and she is still standing.

She never stays in the same place; she advances to the place that God destined for her life. Not everyone is going to accompany her, but she knows that if God is with her, she has everything.

She is the one who knows that every step she takes brings her closer to her destiny, even if she is rejected by others. She is an extraordinary woman.

GOD BECOMES THE SENTINEL OF MAN AND WOMAN, FOR BLESSING OR FOR JUDGMENT

11

> *"You can be disappointed and have a bad marriage, but remember that you are someone and you must gather the courage to make the necessary transitions to a new life."*

I believe that one must understand as a woman the dimension and importance that the marital union has for God.

WOMAN'S GREATEST **FRUSTRATION**

Coming up, I wanted to transcribe a testimony that a woman wrote to me, who for years lived a very difficult story with her husband, despite the fact that he had many opportunities from God to truly change and have a very prosperous life with her and his four children.

Unfortunately, today he is in prison for not giving room to God and all the help that his wife gave him, because even in the midst of so much hatred from him, she always loved him and endured countless humiliations and moments of tremendous pain.

> *This is part of a story where I always saw the hand of God working for good, although I did not understand the reason for the situations. It began when Christ found me after living a married life in sadness and pain. I recognize that when the founder of marriage, who is Jesus Christ of Nazareth, is not present, too many humiliations are suffered.*
>
> *For years I experienced physical, and mainly psychological abuse, to the point that one day after arguing with the father of my children, I left the house crying and went for a walk around the neighborhood where I lived. I still vividly remember wishing a car would hit me, because I didn't want to live anymore. I felt that my life was a life without purpose, I felt that I was not happy, that my world was sad, I felt empty, without love and that no one loved me, and that was my reality.*
>
> *Even though I walked several blocks, no car ever passed by, which seemed very*

GOD BECOMES THE SENTINEL OF MAN AND WOMAN

strange to me, since it was a very busy street. Although at that moment I didn't understand anything, now I know that it was God protecting me from death, because if not, I would now be in hell itself.

As time went by, there was always someone who God used to tell me about His ways, and they told me that God could change my marriage. Although something was happening inside me that gave me encouragement to move forward, our relationship continued from bad to worse.

You may be wondering, why was it so bad? What was happening?

Without knowing the reality of the problem, I discovered that I was living with a person who consumed drugs, which I never found out until years later. Despite the ugly and confusing moments, there was always something that gave me hope that a day would come where everything would change. Of course, in my ignorance I thought it could happen like magic because that's how we women dream it could happen, but it's not like that. If it were not for the hand of God and for his mercy to have found me and planted me in the church, which I bless in the name of Jesus, I would not be telling you this.

I lived in a cosmopolitan city and my plans were not to move, on the contrary, I had plans for my 3 children to grow up and make a life in that state where we lived, but God's plans were very different.

God had planned a true transformation for my life, and one day we moved to a city that I can now say for me is the land flowing with milk and honey.

I was invited to the CODM Church. I will never forget the first day I arrived. The first thing that conquered me was praise; It seemed like angels were the ones singing during the time of worship, and I said to myself: 'this is beautiful, I feel something that I have never experienced', and together with my family we began to attend the CODM Church.

I accepted Christ as my Lord and Savior, and the church was my refuge. In it I found a family, I found love from my Apostles, from their family, I began to feel safe and my inner life began to regain strength.

The most beautiful and best thing I experienced is that I began to feel the love of God. I received the hug of a Father, something I had never experienced, because as a woman, when you get married you expect the man who will be your husband to love you, take care of you and respect you. And how unpleasant it is to experience over the years that it is quite the opposite. Having my husband next to me, but his heart and mind always being in something else or another place, was for me as if he were not there.

I felt ignored, disappointed, but in those moments was where God began to reveal himself to my life. By hearing his Word through messages in church services, I understood that God never leaves us or forsakes us. On the contrary, we leave and ignore, giving way to our self and putting our trust in people, and in my case, in my husband.

God is good, God is great in mercy and if only we put him first, we would not experience so many disappointments, taking into account that He is the only faithful one, the one who does not fail us, the one who does not sleep to take care of us. Glory to God!

On many occasions the father of my children would leave home for any reason. We could have a beautiful day, as a family, but the next day without saying a word, he would leave and be gone for months. That generated a lot of insecurity in me and my children, since without caring if we had rent, food, or even gasoline, he abandoned us to our own fate.

When you are in these situations you feel that you are rowing against the current and that everything is lost, that there is nothing more to do, but there was something in me that told me to persevere in prayer, to continue assisting church and not give up.

Something would happen if I did not faint, and today I remember that on one occasion I went to church and the Apostle approached me and told me to persevere, because I would only be able to see the blessing if I did not faint, and I treasured that in my heart to continue attending the congregation.

One time I only had $20 dollars in my wallet, and it was a church service day. I felt the Holy Spirit telling me to give everything I had and for a moment I thought, "these $20 dollars is all I have," but instantly I said, "God, you own everything I have and everything I am.", and without thinking further, I went and gave my offering.

As I was leaving the church after finishing the service, a woman I didn't know gave me an envelope and told me: "Open it when you get home, and take it because I feel in my heart to give it to you, may God bless you." I did as she requested. When I got home, I told my children: "Look what a lady at church gave me." When I opened it, inside the envelope was a check for US$400.

My tears rolled down my face, I raised my hands to heaven and said, "Lord Jesus, thank you that you have provided for me when I had nothing." These experiences led me to increase my faith and see the care and hand of the Lord over my life and that of my children, and to not waver in my Christian walk.

One of the things that helped me keep standing, was to not stop assisting church. Every time I had situations of rejection or abuse, I ran and held on harder to the hands of Jesus Christ, and by continuing to persevere I was called to service, and that was where I felt most committed to continuing to attend the services of the CODM church.

One day my children's father had an opportunity to move very far from the church, and he told me to get ready because

we were going to move soon. Something in me told me that if I moved, I was going to move away from the place where I felt most safe and protected and it wouldn't be for the best, because let me tell you that I was freed from so many dangers that God kept me safe even from death.
I told him that I was not following him in that plan, because, at that time, the church, the apostolic family, the people of the congregation were very important in my life. I began to look at my apostles, especially, as my parents, not only as my apostles, but I trusted them more than my biological parents.
Thanks to their advice, their example of perseverance, and love for the ministry, they shaped my life to persevere and dream, feeling that God could heal my wounds and that He had the power to heal my husband and have a blessed married life.
I continued to persevere by assisting church and listening to the advice of my apostles, and although there were situations when I wanted to throw in the towel, their love, their advice, and their patience made me understand so many wonderful truths hidden in the Word of God.
I will not deny that leaving everything crossed my mind many times and sometimes I thought about moving to another state and starting a new life, but the church always stopped me; I knew I wouldn't find another one like CODM.
One day the father of my children lied to me.

He told me he was going to work and the truth was different. Although it was nothing new, since he had done it before, feeling betrayed once again was not pleasant. So, I confronted him face to face and told him that I didn't want to live like this anymore, that I was tired of not seeing any positive changes in him and that I didn't want to stay by his side anymore, and crying with my broken heart I told him: 'You will never see me cry again, because it will be the last day you look at me and I talk to you.'

The moment I said those words, I felt the Holy Spirit in my heart so strongly that I spoke to him about forgiveness and led him to ask for forgiveness and forgive those who had wronged him. Although naturally I didn't want to, I had to do it, because it was not me, but the hand and power of God that wanted to heal him. I told him everything that God gave me at that moment, and I know that he would not have done it if it were not for the Holy Spirit. I remember telling him, 'You must forgive whoever has wronged you; God wants to extend His forgiveness to you and show you His love because God loves you.' I gave him a big hug and he started crying.

I remember that my tears began to come because I didn't even believe that after all I was hugging him and saying those words to him, which were not mine. There I was able to see that when God gets involved in our affairs, even if the situation is very big or painful, God always turns it the way He wants.

In conclusion, of the story, I can say from my experience that perseverance in assisting the church where God places us is essential to grow in all areas. No matter how weak you think you are or what terrible situation you may face, there is nothing that God cannot do for you, as long as you persevere in faith and trust that God is the God of the impossible. He is our healer, our liberator, our good Father and because he is our good Father, he blesses us by giving us excellent spiritual parents.

Sowing in the correct ministry and having spiritual coverage is essential to ensure that old and sad things are put aside and one is strengthened through the Word. That is why I can say from my own experience that perseverance is very important to continue moving forward.

I thank God for my apostles, who are extraordinary, enterprising, persevering, truly admirable people. After all these years of persevering, I can say that the Holy Spirit is ready to change the history of your present, take you to a glorious, blessed, prosperous future, so that you can live a life in victory, because with Christ we are more than victors, we are prisoners of hope, and not people who live their lives depending on painful circumstances.

We were all born to succeed, but it would not be achieved without the Word of God, the church, which is the house of prayer and it is very important to have spiritual parents like the ones I have.

I want to tell you who have read this precious testimony that one of the virtues that I can highlight about this dear woman is that she was obedient, persevering, and faithful to God and to us, her spiritual parents.

She is very beautiful and elegant, but she was never unfaithful to her husband, even though everything she experienced could have driven her to do so, but she is a true Christian. Attending church was her most important decision because she always felt cared for, supported and protected.

It is also a model of the decisions that she made, and without failing to respect her husband, she first obeyed God and His ways, taking into account that the Word of God is clear about this. Only when subjection compromises her relationship with God and leads her to sin, a woman is not obligated to obey her husband and she has to obey God first, otherwise she must be faithful to this precept.

Her marriage ended in divorce, but since God is a God of second chances, today she remarried a man who loves her and takes care of her, and he is very affectionate with her and her four children.

Remember that, in second marriages, when there are children from a previous marriage, the man not only marries that woman, but also her children, and must be responsible for those lives.

You can be disappointed and have a bad marriage, but remember that you are someone and you must gather the courage to make the necessary transitions to a new life.

With God you never lose, with God you always win.

12 THE GOD OF THE MOUNTAINS IS ALSO THE GOD OF THE VALLEYS

"Dear woman: there will be times when you will have to take refuge in the heart of God, because He operates in us by His Power."

We all experience emotional ups and downs. You work and work until you are exhausted, with so much anguish and sorrow. When you are up, happiness and joy fill your heart, but when you are in the valley, sadness and loneliness fill your entire being.

When you cultivate a place for spiritual rest in your inner being, you strengthen yourself and protect your soul from falling into a deep pit, because let's agree that it is very easy to get depressed and so difficult to get out of that situation.

It's true, we get tired, we wear ourselves out day by

day, month after month, year after year. But look how extraordinary. Your life does not depend on the circumstances you are going through, but on the God whom you serve. Perhaps, you as a woman hope to be lifted up and supported by those around you; husband, children, family, friends. However, there will be times when you will have to take refuge in the heart of God, because He operates in us by His Power.

> **YOUR LIFE DOES NOT DEPEND ON THE CIRCUMSTANCES YOU ARE GOING THROUGH, BUT ON THE GOD WHOM YOU SERVE.**

How would you feel if I told you that Someone has already suffered for you so that you would be better? Jesus Christ of Nazareth. This biblical passage is extraordinary:

> *Now all glory to God, who is able, through his mighty power at work within us, to accomplish infinitely more than we might ask or think. (Ephesians 3:20, NLT).*

Analyzing this biblical passage, ask yourself: Why are you always asking people for what you can ask of the Lord, if the Word of God says that even when we ask God, He has the power to do much more than what you ask of Him... if we are complete in Him? Furthermore, he says that: But, as it is written, *"What no eye has seen, nor ear heard, nor the heart of man imagine, what God has prepared for those who love him" (1 Corinthians 2:9, ESV).*

All knowledge we have of God is spiritual, and from there it is revealed to our spirit, through the Holy Spirit. That is why it says that we cannot even imagine what God can help us with his power, since we are talking about the Almighty God creator of the universe, and even the hidden treasures and closely guarded secrets will manifest through those of us who seek his face.

Therefore, you must understand that, having cemented your faith in the Lord, and being sustained by the Power of His Word, whatever situation you go through, be it up the mountain or down in the valley, you are spiritually sustained in prayer and communion with God. From there, you will see how your life with that man who frustrates you and sometimes you don't know what to do becomes more bearable.

Intercede for that man who makes you live on a kind of roller coaster, one day up, another day down, with childish and unexpected behaviors; with unexpected and capricious reactions, that simply surprise you and throw you off.

But there are truths planned in the mind of God to be poured out into the lives of God's daughters. I am constantly amazed to see how the Lord brings so much clarity to our minds in such a specific way. That's why you should ignore those comments that divert you from the truth about yourself.

Let go of the accusations and insults that conflict with the Lord's will for your future. Seek God's attention towards you, and not that of men, then, you will find true well-being for your soul, stillness and rest in your spirit.

Understand that no one changes

UNDERSTAND THAT NO ONE CHANGES ANYONE, ONLY GOD CAN DO IT.

anyone, only God can do it, that is why I always tell women: "Say out loud to your husband: My love, I am leaving you in peace, may the Lord change you." You give Him a kiss and you fall asleep peacefully knowing that He will do it.

Now, while it is true that all women need to be valued and once that happens, we learn to dream, I want to teach you how important it is to fulfill God's calling for your life. We have always heard that women have many abilities and talents, but if this is not put at the service of the Lord and his work, and God's calling for our lives is unfulfilled, everything you do will be fruitless.

Knowing that you were predestined for this time to proclaim a truth, the truth of the Gospel of Jesus Christ. This will give you self-confidence and when you speak you will transmit harmony.

I wish that everything you do is driven by love, joy and a life completely surrendered to God, because when you bring to the world the treasure you carry within you, everything around you will suffer opposition. However, once God's blessing is released, it will be superabundant and reach every sphere of your life. Extraordinary.

LOVE BEGINS IN THE KITCHEN

13

"Everything you do as a woman strengthening emotional bonds will culminate in tremendous personal satisfaction, accepting who you really are and the powerful influence you exert on others."

He may not find everything he is looking for in the refrigerator, because he stands staring for a long time looking for what you asked him to help you in the kitchen. Maybe he will ask you once again how the microwave works yet take the initiative to cook together.

Always remember that he wants to stand out for you and feel important and necessary, because, although you are a competent woman and skilled at making recipes for the whole family, accepting his ideas to cook something new and distinct will make you share something different.

My husband had to learn many things from a very young age and one of them was cooking, although (I admit) he irons clothes better than me, he is very organized and neat, and I like that when he cooks, he gives a different savor to the meals. Although I suggest some things to him, I take advantage of the time he cooks to do the things I like, like writing.

Think about this: do you worry so much about how he will make the food, if the food is served on the table?

I remember when I made my first meal for my husband and of course, to this day he remembers it and always tells it as an anecdote and not because the recipe was well made, but because that stew came out so dry that when he mentions it, we can't stop laughing. But we were passionate and ate it as if it were an extraordinary delicacy.

One of the best things I can say here is that we have always been very happy, with little or more, but enjoying being together.

Now, one has to understand that not every day you will be inspired to be a chef of haute cuisine, but you do have to understand the reason for the famous phrase: "love begins in the kitchen." Several studies have been carried out that prove that cooking is good therapy for couples. In addition, it makes them accomplices and companions because they are sharing an activity where they must create something together: a recipe.

There you will see how emotional ties are strengthened. That is why it is so powerful that you have that valuable time in your daily life to enjoy those small moments where you will laugh, chat and, above all, share anecdotes and memories from the past. Now to eat what was created, which will fill you with satisfaction and joy for what you have done together!

Keep in mind that everything in daily life that makes you work as a team will culminate in better intimacy for the couple, because it is impossible for nice words and flirting not to arise between both of you while you are cooking.

Women often downplay the importance of sexual life, without understanding that this is man's first need, because God made him that way, whether you like it or not. Therefore, love begins in the kitchen and culminates in the bedroom. So, you are happy because he helped you cook, taking a big burden off your shoulders, and he receives the reward for having been so detailed in doing a task that often seems so tedious to us.

I read that The Washington Post has described that couples who share household chores, including cooking, have a better relationship, sex life, and long-term life. The latter caught my attention: "long-term life." There is a tendency to live day to day with one's own concerns, but one must stop and strengthen the couple with an eye toward the future.

Sharing, sharing that is the secret of success with the man who lives with you, giving him the first place in your life, and I say this knowing that there are women who cry out loud when they hear these words for fear of losing their place. They are women who give priority to their children, not considering that they are passing through your life, because the one you will share the rest of your days with is your husband.

Therefore, everything you do as a

SHARING, SHARING THAT IS THE SECRET OF SUCCESS WITH THE MAN WHO LIVES WITH YOU.

woman strengthening emotional ties will culminate in tremendous personal satisfaction, accepting who you really are and the powerful influence you exert on others.

There is always time for everything, even to stop doing those things that you consider "important", but that will not contribute anything to your future. Think about it. Doing nothing is also healthy. Sitting in your garden or in your favorite chair and letting others do what you do, "because no one does it better than you…" is strengthening for your physical and mental health.

Rest, woman, rest in the fact that he will do it, because the backpack that you carry on your back, it is time for you to leave it, to combine goals and objectives with the person with whom one day you fell in love, but that the tedious routine and work have made you lose sight of what was important: emotional stability.

The more time you share things with your man, the more fulfilled you will feel. Tell him your most intimate secrets, which will forge a greater affinity between you. Everything you want to know about him that he doesn't tell you, from now on he will and thus there will be greater communication and understanding between the both of you. Trust is the main thing in a relationship, and it is achieved by you taking the first step. You will get to know him so much that you will know when to speak and when to be silent and pray, which is powerful. It will help you stay silent when it is wise to do so, and you will see how much trouble you will avoid.

If you are a woman who has vast knowledge about many things, and you have lived experiences regarding your family's health, household finances or what is related to your profession, try not to give him lessons on these topics, especially when he is wrong. Let it go and in the moment he least notices, you tell him. That works better than arguing without reaching an agreement.

Ah... When you ask him to cook together you show him that you are not self-sufficient, that you can let yourself be helped, since he likes to be kind and show you that he is your partner in everything.

THE BIBLE SAYS THAT THE WOMAN IS THE "WEAKER VESSEL," WHICH MEANS THAT MAN IS ALSO FRAGILE.

The Bible says that the woman is the "weaker vessel," which means that man is also fragile. Therefore, your sensitivity will help you decipher his emotional state.

> *Likewise, husbands, live with your wives in an understanding way, showing honor to the woman as the weaker vessel, since they are heirs with you of the grace of life, so that your prayers may not be hindered. (1 Peter 3:7, ESV)*

Like a weaker vessel you must allow yourself to be kept and protected by the Lord because no one uses a cracked or dirty glass to pour clean water, so your life must always be purified by the Word of God. You must become a restored woman, and there you will be able to clearly hear the voice of God, understanding that what you do in Him you will do through His Power and not your own strength.

It is your essence that becomes valuable, and you will open your ears to hear the voice of God, which is extraordinary because you will leave your natural inclination to do things and do them with your spirit.

Imagine something as simple as the act of cooking together, and ending up concluding that it will bring something more than that, as a powerful union between the two of you. A new way of seeing things must manifest in you and be a good influence on others.

14
LET YOURSELF BE FORMED BY HIM

I read this phrase on an Instagram page called: "A Couple with a Purpose": "The wife should strive for her husband to be happy when he gets home, and the husband should strive that she is sorry to see him leave".

It is so motivating for the man that you tell him often how much you love him and how you like to spend time with him and feel his hugs and caresses. I know you're thinking he doesn't do that very often. You wonder why he isn't more affectionate with you, even though you love seeing him a little different on certain occasions.

Let me tell you a story and you will understand that you can take the first step to then receive the reward for your actions.

> IT IS SO MOTIVATING FOR THE MAN THAT YOU TELL HIM OFTEN HOW MUCH YOU LOVE HIM.

Man has the ability to lead, he always wants to be the boss. Therefore, where there is a boss, there is another who obeys, and this is where the difficulties begin, where the greatest crises occur. That is why the title of this chapter is: Let yourself be formed by him. In other words, hand the baton over to him.

In the Bible we find the story of Queen Esther, who just before becoming queen she had to do several things to achieve her promotion. Esther's first step was to enter the palace and purify herself for a year before seeing the king.

> *The young women were given beauty treatments for one whole year. The first six months their skin was rubbed with olive oil and myrrh, and the last six months it was treated with perfumes and cosmetics. Then each of them spent the night alone with King Xerxes. When a young woman went to the king, she could wear whatever clothes or jewelry she chose from the women's living quarters. (Esther 2:12-13, CEV)*

Note that before appearing before the king and considering that she could be chosen as the queen consort, she was prepared for a whole year. In that area, women were prone to having very dry skin considering that there was a lot of dust, poor diet and heat that wreaked havoc on women's skin. They had to go through a deep beautification and hygiene process just to appear before the king.

On the other hand, Esther was an orphan raised by her cousin and forcibly taken to the king's women's house, with the possibility of being rejected and left as a widow within the same harem, without the hope of being able to marry, because that was the end of the remaining women who were not chosen. However, look at what happened:

> *Xerxes liked Esther more than he did any of the other young women. None of them pleased him as much as she did, and he immediately fell in love with her and crowned her queen in place of Vashti. (Esther 2:17, CEV)*

Here I want to highlight two virtues that Esther developed: grace and benevolence. She was very obedient throughout that year to the eunuch who oversaw her preparation.

For a woman to have grace is primarily the favor of God on her life.
On the other hand, the beauty of a woman is a determining factor in being chosen and being the only one for that man who loves her, because let's agree once again that a man sees everything through his eyes; God made him that way.

There was a strong decision on Ester's part in this story to prepare herself and allow herself to be molded by the entire structure of that time, which, if we think about it, practically the same thing happens today. The woman who is not prepared, who is not updated, and fashionable is a woman who can lose in the face of so much competition.

She had to stand out among four hundred women, but Esther had inner beauty. She was a woman of dignity… strength and bravery. Esther was a girl who stood out. Her character was worthy of admiration. Her character earned her the grace and goodwill of everyone. She had a spirit that attracted…

There are women who make bad decisions and without realizing it, they distance that man from their lives with manipulation and whims. That is why you should always find a way to observe him with eyes of love and stimulate him with beautiful words; it is what will make you a better woman for him. You must pay attention to him, since he is not just another piece of furniture in your house, and he is so sensitive that he needs your admiration in everything he does and your smiles when he makes a mistake or does something wrong.

Furthermore, let us be aware that there are things that we can change and others that we cannot; you must settle and move forward. You should always be his biggest attraction. I always say that if the devil doesn't kill you spiritually, he does it by destroying you physically. Our good health as women will allow us not only to be attractive in all areas for that man, but it will extend our life so we can enjoy future generations.

LET THE LITTLE THINGS GO TO FOCUS ON ALL THE GOOD THINGS THAT MAN HAS.

Let yourself be formed by him while not losing your identity, because your identity does matter. Let the little things go to focus on all the good things that man has, because no one forced you to marry him, and if you did it wrongly and just out of passion, it is never too late to change and help the other make changes, above all if there are children involved.

There is a saying that says: "If one does not want to, two cannot…" and if you are willing, there is a God who tells you: "I will help you…"

LET YOURSELF BE FORMED BY HIM

You will not be alone in this process, it simply requires you to bend your will and learn to give in, and I want to highlight this because it is something that is very difficult for women.

Remember something I already told you: let go of your husband, throw a kiss in the air and say: "I can't do more, may God change you…". Then you give him over to the Lord and He can do in a second what took you years trying.

There is a Psalm that has helped me a lot throughout my life, and it is Psalm 46:10, in its first part it says: Be still, and know that I am God; …
Stop, meditate, and wait…do not be anxious, because it is God himself making this promise to you. Trust that He and only He will do it and it truly does happen.

Look at this wonderful Word of the Lord:

> *It shall also come to pass that before they call, I will answer; and while they are still speaking, I will hear. (Isaiah 65:24, AMP)*

God Himself is watching over you and asks you to put yourself in His blessed hands because He will not allow a single hair to fall from your head without Him knowing it. He is such a detailed God, such a loving Father, that all we must do is trust, trust and believe, that He will do it. I have seen his actions many times in my life, which is why I leave you this extraordinary Word. Make it yours when critical moments come, and you will unleash the potential that is in you.

I have noticed that the more docile I am with my husband, the less problems I have, and in all these years I have been very obedient. I have carried all those things that have not seemed good to me in prayer and have observed the hand of God in everything. Amid all the situations there were things that were torn down and then we decided to build together, just him and me. We did not allow our children or close relatives to intervene.

On one occasion, an incident arose with an aunt who wanted to impose her opinion and want my husband to do things the way she said, and since she couldn't do it, she asked me to side with her in what she was saying and contradicted my husband. Since I didn't do it, she approached me with great anger and told me the following: "You are not a woman!"

I felt a lot of pain at the time because of her words, but the years passed and seeing the success in our marriage, one day she remembered her words, asked for my forgiveness, and told me: "You truly are an excellent woman".

Your actions and the result of them will be your best endorsement in front of people. Permanence over time, despite the circumstances, is what will speak highly of you and your good attitudes.

GUILTY, WHO? I? 15

The first thing I want to tell you is that all women always carry some guilt. The origin is always related to things that we cannot fulfill. Let me tell you that it comes from childhood with parents who were very demanding and rigid. We maintain that attitude of always wanting to please others, that you should not be selfish and sacrificially put the desires of others before your own (whether it be your husband, children, parents, or in-laws).

The situations that are experienced "without realizing it" are those in which no harm was truly intended, and this tends to happen very often in women who, because they have their minds on so many activities, make this type of mistake. The consequences are that that husband no longer believes her because he thinks that she "did it on purpose." There is a lot of hostility towards her, and her feelings begin to change.

On her side, she feels so dissatisfied with herself that the guilt now grows, and she reproaches herself for having done it, wishing to go back in time. Isn't that true?

Result of guilt: Not having become the person one could have been. But that is impossible, what is possible is to take steps of faith little by little, to reverse that situation. This verse struck me:

> *By this we shall know that we are of the truth and reassure our heart before him; for whenever our heart condemns us, God is greater than our heart, and he knows everything. (1 John 3:19-20, ESV)*

Accusations against us are common. Look at this example: Satan tempted Eve because he knew she was more vulnerable to attack, and she had not received the command from God not to eat from the tree, but from Adam.

Therefore, although it was always believed that it was Eve's fault for falling into her temptation, in reality the person responsible for her was Adam because he had to take care of her. Many of the accusations against women are the responsibility of men, to whom God will ask an account of.

However, notice how wonderful God is that even when you condemn yourself, He does not reject you, on the contrary, you always remain his daughter. He will always recognize your merits and your values.

Feelings of guilt

> *But he answered them, "You see all these, do you not? Truly, I say to you, there will not be left here one stone upon another that will not be thrown down". (Matthew 24:2, ESV)*

Jesus said this. The feeling of guilt makes people not live in true freedom. It is a stone in your life. It is an anchor that stops you and does not let you move forward, when many times they are ethical questions of no seriousness.

You must decide to truly forgive those who hurt you, but mainly yourself; to say, "well, that's it, today I decide to forgive, I'm not going to walk with this anymore in my life, today I truly forgive myself."

Jesus already forgave us. He is willing to heal you internally from the feeling of guilt, but you are the one who must make the decision. Are you one of those who defend themselves?

> **THE FEELING OF GUILT MAKES PEOPLE NOT LIVE IN TRUE FREEDOM.**

I reiterate that there are situations over which you do not have control but how wonderful it is when you hand it over to God. He solves it and you rest knowing that you are in the best hands. Because He clothes us with His Righteousness, and He sees us as holy and blameless as His son Jesus Christ. Marvelous.

Are you one of those who doesn't let someone else make decisions for you? In marriage we must be submitted and committed, because it is the man who must take his place and be the one who leads us, who takes responsibility and takes the baton of command.

Hebrews 4:16 tells us:

> *Let us then with confidence draw near to the throne of grace, that we may receive mercy and find grace to help in time of need.*

The enemy will always come to accuse you, but the Lord comes into our lives to comfort us. Finally, anything that is not in line with Scripture did not originate in the heart of God. Therefore, accusations must be answered because the enemy's intention is to torment you with feelings of guilt.

But how good it is to know that there is a throne of grace and not of punishment, because men want to punish you, but God gives you his mercy for the deeds of your past, and grace for the present and future.
So, approach God with frankness, without reservations, because the Word always reveals our condition to us, but without a doubt it is for our good.

16
COMPLICATED WOMEN

"If everything bothers you it is because you are a suffocating woman, and you have to have a change of attitude."

It has always been said that "there is an air of mystery" in women and that men say that they are "difficult to understand and predict".

I want to tell you something very important: attitude in life is everything.
Depending on your attitude is what will make that man approach you or distance from you. (Although sometimes you can't stand him, and you don't know how to get him out of your life).

ATTITUDE IN LIFE IS EVERYTHING.

If you are one of those women who gets annoyed by everything, because the child is making a lot of noise, because your husband always leaves everything lying around, because the traffic light takes a long time to change, because the supermarket cashier is late... if everything bothers you, it is because you are a suffocating woman and you have to have a change of attitude. That's what I'm going to talk to you about from now on.

Talking to my daughter Daniela about the situations that arise daily with people who love you today and despise you tomorrow, she told me this phrase: "There are people who are not part of my life." I found so much truth in this. They are part of your story, but they are not aligned with your destiny.

That's the defensive attitude that people and even your husband develop when you're a complicated woman like the one I've described.

It is incredible that there are people, and women specifically, who, even if they are Christians, we can never merge with them; first they love you and then they can't even see you. The most incredible thing is that one knows perfectly well that nothing bad has been done to them, quite the opposite. They are people who don't fit in with you and never will. Difficult, right? That's the fickle, complicated woman whose attitude harms her marriage.

> **THE WAY YOU APPROACH THE DAY IS HOW YOU WILL LIVE IT.**

However, I rescue a phrase from a letter from a young woman who wrote me the following on my birthday: "Appreciating you, my spiritual parents, is as if I appreciated the very presence of God and honoring you both is as if I could give a gift to Jesus Christ himself".

Observe with me the following. Like this woman, there are so many others who appreciate spiritual help and value advice and put it into practice, while others totally despise the good that you tell them. This is where we must understand that not all people want to change. There are situations where they have become so accustomed to the bad that they cannot appreciate anything good in their life. That is another of the behaviors of a complicated woman. When it is time to bond with someone like this, learn to separate yourself when it is necessary to do so, so that you do not become contaminated by her attitude.

We said that attitude is everything in life. The way you approach the day is how you will live it. With God it is so easy, He tells you:

> *If you will seek God and plead with the Almighty for mercy… (Job 8:5)*
> *O God, you are my God; earnestly I seek you;… (Psalm 63:1)*

Those women who seek God early, get out of bed and say like King David:

> *This is the day that the Lord has made; let us rejoice and be glad in it. (Psalm 118:24)*

It is so positive and energizing to give thanks for each day, honor the life the Lord allows us to live, and be a blessing to others. Then there is no one who can be against us; get ready because you will be surprised by God.

Are you one of those who apologizes often?

Come on, let's be honest and agree that we are so proud,

and we believe we know it all. "And if you don't win, you draw…" but never give in. However, life is much calmer when you learn to give in, to say "I'm sorry", "I was wrong". But never say, "I didn't realize…" That is a terrible phrase.

Your attitude towards disputes and disagreements are your decision. Many times, you will have to be silent and just pray; these are just moments and better things are coming.

Learn to ask for forgiveness; it is so healing, because you get those you hold prisoner out of jail. Most likely, while he doesn't even realize it, he goes about his day, and you are there suffering and crying. Live forgiving, letting go and being truly free.

FROM LOVE TO HATE 17

> *"Never allow your heart to be flooded with hatred. Keep the good things about the other person and forget all the bad things they made you suffer. Throw away bad thoughts and end your past".*

As the years go by in your married life, you will change, and your husband will change too. No one is prepared for these changes, especially if they have been together for many years. Control over the other is not only exercised by men; women do it too, demanding that he continue with the same sensitivity and humor they had when they first fell in love.

Everything "wild" that the relationship had, today is monotony and boredom because the ability to listen to the other, to understand them, is gone, and this is daily.

Familiarity makes that "gentleman" who was previously all romanticism, today only have complaints and reproaches towards you and your children. He seems irritated and dissatisfied with you, and you wonder what wrong you have done to him to make him react like this.

If you are separated by a trip, you don't miss him because you no longer have that constant voice hammering you day after day with demands of what he wanted to see in you and expressed to you with so much hatred that you ask yourself: "Have I lived with this man to this day?" and "Weren't we going to be happy forever?"

It's so sad when you think that you said, "I do" and now you don't accept him anymore. Between the disagreements and the turbulence, you begin to feel hate, yes, hate, when you had loved him so much.

So, this is where the decision begins, to seek the love of God like never before because you are halfway there and you must keep walking, because marriage is a commitment. And love is unconditional.

THROW AWAY BAD THOUGHTS AND END YOUR PAST.

Never allow your heart to be flooded with hate. Keep the good things about the other person and forget all the bad things they made you suffer. Throw away bad thoughts and end your past.

Hatred comes from Satan himself, who injects ideas into our minds, filling it with confusion and many times situations arise that are not real, so we must reject all "vain imagination," as the Bible says.

The reality is that hate always harms us because it steals inner peace and joy and has a negative effect on our physical well-being. Hate will make you lose sleep and even your appetite, deteriorating your health.

We must empty ourselves

There is something very powerful that I want to teach you and that at one point in my life also worked for me, and it is the power of emptying ourselves. Yes, emptying ourselves because our inner being is so full of so many burdens, feelings and experiences that have to do with our past and God does not look at our past, He is our future.

We must abandon that desire to always be "doing something." There is so much power in rest, in getting away to a secret place and seeking the Holy Spirit to fill you. But, of course, one cannot be filled if one is not first emptied, because it is not that we cannot be filled, but that there are no empty spaces into which the Holy Spirit can enter.

There are strongholds that have made you miss the mark: pride, arrogance, hidden jealousy, obsessive thoughts, emotional wounds. Remember that most women come before the Lord spiritually damaged and physically weary; and God has to deal with every area of mental stronghold so that those areas be emptied out.

The Holy Spirit will only fill spaces that are empty. And we must do this constantly to be able to advance in all areas of our life. It is not possible to be emptied at once and then be filled forever. Remember this.

BEFORE YOU GET DIVORCED... THINK TWICE

18

In this chapter you will read the most interesting story you have ever read in your life. Pay a lot of attention:

One day your husband comes, and he asks you for a separation. Furthermore, he tells you that he does not intend to change his mind, that he has made his decision. And you who thought you had married for life. I want to tell you a story:
"Mike was a family man; he had been married to Jessica for 23 years and they had four children together. They had known each other since their youth and were very close. He was a psychologist and she had studied the same career with him, but she was dedicated to raising their four children.

Like every year, they go on vacation to a very popular beach and there he begins to have a love affair with Ashley, a very pretty woman ten years younger than him, also married, but with a marriage already destroyed.

The dazzle and passion that was unleashed between them

was such that they both separated from their respective spouses and went to live together. At the same time and after getting divorced, Mike and Ashley got married. Everything seemed so wonderful and new between them that all they did was live this new stage in their lives with great intensity.

Needless to say, both Mike's wife and Ashley's husband suffered tremendously from the betrayal of their respective partners, but as time passed, they had a second chance and got married.

Both Mike and Ashley remained together in their new marriage for three years, and after this time she filed for divorce because he lived from one affair to another.

The interesting thing about this story is that one day Ashley and Jessica meet at a cafe and sat down to chat. In the middle of a pleasant conversation between the two, Jessica, Mike's first wife, asks her: "What was he like with you? How can you describe him?" Ashley responds: "captivating, very bright, intense, and impulsive; very ambitious, but he was very mature. He was a man who took care of things around the house and my life."

Jessica, Mike's first wife, looks at her in amazement and tells her: "I always saw him as insecure, obviously very intelligent, but I was always after him to take care of family matters and work." Jessica looks Ashley in the eyes and says, "I think people see what they want to see in other people. You know? "I always thought he wasn't really yours," Jessica tells her, "That I was lending him to you until he got tired and decided to come back even after he married you".

With tears in her eyes, Ashley tells her: "I'm sorry, Jessica, for what I did to you, he was your husband, you were married and had children."

This is the lesson I want to leave you from this story. Jessica ends by telling Ashley: "Look, but it's not your fault, men have to feel important to stay in a relationship, and I stopped making him feel important years before he noticed you. "Don't blame yourself about what happened".

She stopped making her husband feel important. She took care of herself, her children, her business, her parents, but the last thing she took care of was the most important person in the home: the man. There are women who are frustrated in their marriage, but they do not realize that there is a serious mistake they are making, and its priorities.

> **MEN HAVE TO FEEL IMPORTANT TO STAY IN A RELATIONSHIP.**

Separation in couples occurs for many reasons, but I want to focus on the consequences that are unleashed in this process. I know thousands of cases where after a decision as determinant as separating, it specifically produces fear, failure, and depression in the woman.

I want to be very objective but saying: "I am married" is not the same as saying: "I am divorced." It is always a shadow of failure, a sad and painful adjective. I want to share the following with you:

Ten commandments for wives

1. Always be kind and sensitive to your husband.

2. Be your husband's biggest fan.

3. Never give him lessons. If you don't agree, wait, and let God deal with it.

4. Never scold him! You are his wife, not his mother.

5. Show him off to your friends and family. Honor him publicly.

6. Make him his favorite dish, turn off the light, uncork a bottle of champagne and sprinkle on some Christian Dior at least once a week.

7. Throw away that robe! Yes, just that. Wear something nice and never wear curlers, especially in bed.

8. Tell him how proud you are of him (especially in front of his children).

9. Never take someone's side against your husband. Always be by his side, especially when he makes mistakes.

10. Tell him often that you respect and love him.
You can be a good woman, or you can be a great woman. You choose, because you are there to ease man's burdens.

FIDELITY IS A VIRTUE 19

"Your main ministry as a wife is not in the ladies' group, in your children's school or in the church, it is in your home together with your husband."

When you decide to enter a committed relationship with a man, you have to understand that there must be exclusivity between the two of you. The woman needs to know that she is the only woman in that man's life, although the man may not have the same need. He may have a wife at home and one or more lovers outside, and he acts in such a natural way leading a double life that no matter how much his wife complains to him, since he does not pass everything through his feelings, he continues living as if nothing had happened, while his wife suffers permanently.

> **THE WOMAN NEEDS TO KNOW THAT SHE IS THE ONLY WOMAN IN THAT MAN'S LIFE.**

Let us keep in mind that this is not a time in which fidelity is a virtue, quite the opposite. Today the message is "live how you want", "do what you feel" or "feel free".

Beyond all temporal pleasure, this is nothing more than a "false freedom," because the first thing one must have is fidelity to God. Many people wonder where God is, but it turns out that they've left God out of their lives. And as long as the Lord is not part of your life, there will be no fidelity towards anyone, not towards your spouse, nor in any other type of relationship.

The Scriptures tell us all the time about the happiness and peace found in having a good relationship with God. It leads us to understand that we will enjoy well-being and an intimate communion with the Creator. The truth of God's Word is something you can trust your life to.

King David, after committing adultery, always mentioned in the Psalms that he wrote that the truth of the Word preserved him, and that apart from Him he desired nothing more on earth. The entire Psalm 119 is an exaltation of the inescapable truth of the Word of God, irrefutable and powerful to keep us in complete fidelity to Him.

> *I will meditate on your precepts and fix my eyes on your ways. (Psalm 119:15, ESV)*

Remembering the Word of God in certain life situations protects man from falling into a sinful relationship, and from living from deception to deception. It will open his eyes and give him understanding of what he is doing wrong as Psalm 119:10 and 11 says:

> *With my whole heart I seek you; let me not wander from your commandments! I have stored up your word in my heart, that I might not sin against you.*

Having the practice of memorizing the Scriptures will save you from suffering so much pain and sadness. Therefore, my advice is that every man and woman should practice obedience to the Word of God.

If man lived a life totally apart from God and serving the enemy, why does he believe that he has to have access to heaven, a place of such holiness, the day he dies?
I share this verse:

> *Be watchful, stand firm in the faith, act like men, be strong. (1 Corinthians 16:13, ESV)*

The Lord is happy when a man decides to put his faith in Him and allow his life to be transformed. And who better than you, his wife, to help him. Considering how important spiritual intimacy is in marriage, there must be a permanent search for a relationship with God in the both of you. You must know how to measure, as with a thermometer, at what degree of spiritual level each of you find yourselves in, because by having a true relationship with God you will be less likely to argue and get angry, because it is understood that the Holy Spirit dwells in both of you and you must always seek the reconciliation.

Look how wonderful it is to know this: the spiritual life produces true intimacy in all areas and a union of soul to soul, and I say this from experience of many years of marriage. In fact, my husband and I always say that there comes a time when you get to know each other

> **THE SPIRITUAL LIFE PRODUCES TRUE INTIMACY IN ALL AREAS AND A UNION OF SOUL TO SOUL.**

so much that you focus on the other and reach a deep level of intimacy. That is, by making others happy, you receive happiness. God made it this way, that man and woman find great satisfaction in sexual life, and it begins with...

Intimate conversations

Dear woman, you who is reading this book, you must understand that for men sex is very important and if you are interested in this more than anything else, and you are the one who initiates it, you have a lot going for you. This is a topic that must be understood very well because there is a lot of ignorance and underestimation, when in reality sex was established by God himself for marriage.

The male desire for sex is different from that of the female. While for her it is related to the affective, emotional, and sentimental, for him it is a physiological need. Keep in mind that sexual relations produce not only physical, but also emotional and spiritual well-being in men.

The greatest satisfaction for a man is that his wife is interested and motivated every day and however many times to have intimate relations. This increases his masculinity and strengthens the marriage bond. You cannot love your husband and reject him sexually. That causes great harm to him, because sex is an important part of his identity (God made him that way), even though you have different needs. My desire is to help you understand your husband and not argue about those "differences".

Pornography or lust should never be justified, but it is the woman who must be wise in this regard and understand that she must be willing to have intimacy with her husband. In my first book I wrote about the physical and emotional benefits of sexual relations between spouses. Now I add this:

Sex is health

Apart from strengthening the marriage relationship, sex helps you stay fit and keep your heart healthy. It is not a substitute for an exercise routine, but with half an hour of sex you can burn calories. Your body is activated as if you were doing aerobic exercise, and blood circulation and oxygen circulate throughout your body. The lungs are oxygenated, your blood pressure drops, and your posture improves.

When you have an orgasm, large amounts of a hormone called oxytocin are released, which has several effects on the body: it reduces stress and makes you feel revitalized, it helps you sleep and rest better, and added to another hormone called endorphin, it makes the sensation of pain decrease, especially headaches, arthritis and those caused by the symptoms of Premenstrual Syndrome (PMS).

In women, it could help regulate the menstrual cycle and aid in urinary control by keeping the pelvic muscles toned. While, in the case of men, sex can reduce the risk of developing prostate cancer.

As if all this were not enough, sex improves the body's defenses. In this regard, there is research that shows that having sex two or three times a week increases antibodies. Apparently, our body develops them as a preventive measure, since during the sexual act there is an important exchange of bacteria.[2]

---

[2] *Viewed online: https://www.ohsu.edu/womens-health/benefits-healthy-sex-life.*

Remember that when it comes to sex there is so much to learn and change, and you should ask yourself how important sex is to you in your life. Do you relate it to love and pleasure, or do you feel powerful and use it as a weapon to achieve things?

One of the most common situations I have seen in counseling given to women is that if a man who is not her husband says nice words to her, she may fantasize about an unpermitted romance. The Bible clearly states that spouses must be available to each other, and further adds that the woman's body belongs to the man and vice versa.

God's Word is so clear:

> *Husbands and wives should be fair with each other about having sex. A wife belongs to her husband instead of to herself, and a husband belongs to his wife instead of to himself. So don't refuse sex to each other, unless you agree not to have sex for a little while, in order to spend time in prayer. Then Satan won't be able to tempt you because of your lack of self-control. (I Corinthians 7:3-5, CEV)*

Only through you, woman, can that man keep his sexual integrity within the parameters of marriage, and although each one is responsible for their actions, the woman is very important for his containment and satisfaction. Sexual relations are for two, and you both must enjoy. This is why communication and being understanding of each other is so important.

Express your desires with confidence, be very open and

sincere with him, because sexual relations require a lot of energy and you should feel satisfied, contained, and happy.

Your best ministry as a wife is not in the ladies' group, in your children's school or in the church, it is in your home together with your husband.

Your best ministry as a wife is not in the ladies' group, in your children's school or in the church, it is in your home together with your husband.

HE DID IT TO ME... I'LL DO IT WORSE TO HIM

20

> *"In every man there is a good side that must be found. There are good men and women don't see it."*

There are women who disrespect or reject their husbands for actions or characteristics that he cannot change, they come with their own way of being. In a few words: "he is like that…"

We are not equal, which does not lead us to have unity. Having unity does not mean that in marriage we must be the same. Each of us individually has virtues and strengths that help us complement each other. There are good men and women don't see it.

I read this in a book:

> *"Our desire is for our marriage to be the place of our comfort, solace, and delight;*

we usually don't have bigger desires than these. But God's purpose is for each of our marriages to be a tool for something that is far more miraculous and glorious than our small, self-centered definition of happiness. He has designed marriage to be one of his most effective tools of personal holiness. He has designed marriage to change us".³

Phew! Is this so?
Life is lived in moments, there are good and bad, and one of the most difficult relationships is marriage, because you will have to retain the good and discard the bad.
There are experiences that will remain imprinted in your mind and will take a while to erase, and others that you will forget immediately because you will have greater confidence in yourself. That security will help you get ahead in any circumstance, be it illness, separations, abuse, or financial problems.

> **IN EVERY MAN THERE IS A GOOD SIDE THAT MUST BE FOUND.**
>
>

I have always believed that in every man there is a good side that must be found. As I said before, there are good men and women don't see it.

We must always consider the background from which he comes, that is, his upbringing, but the good influence that the woman exerts collaborates in the change that must occur, because not everything we received from our parents was good.

---

³ "What Were You Waiting For?: Redeeming the Realities of Marriage" by Paul David Tripp. Scribd.

HE DID IT TO ME... I'LL DO IT WORSE TO HIM

Every person is "born" and then "made." To what? To the culture and upbringing that he receives, because some within their own home have been told "become a man." True? Man, if he wants, can change, but it remains within him, because I always say, "no one changes anyone." There must be determination and desire to change, which you, woman, can help him. But the attitude of "he did it to me, I'll do it worse to him" perpetuates hatred and resentment, and you will never move forward.

Remember that I am helping you through this book to get out of your frustration.

You must make him understand how you feel at certain moments, because I know of many cases where the husband did not realize what was happening to his wife until the situation was no longer going any further and there was no turning back. Timely dialogue, accurate communication, the right moments to talk will bring a lot of clarity to your lives and your relationship. Something he should know is that you as a woman will always have more in your favor than him in feelings, because through control nothing is achieved, that is, no one is loved by force.

> **TIMELY DIALOGUE, ACCURATE COMMUNICATION, THE RIGHT MOMENTS TO TALK WILL BRING A LOT OF CLARITY TO YOUR LIVES AND YOUR RELATIONSHIP.**

A good man recognizes his dependence on God, values and respects others and does not exercise dominion over people. He is humble.

You are a good woman, and you must have a good man by your side, otherwise you must withdraw in time from a conflictive and violent relationship.

Whenever there is risk in your life, woman, you must think about yourself and your children for whom you do not want that type of situation and make the right decision.
For every pain there is a cure, and God will give you the balm of the oil of compassion to heal the wounds of your husband's heart.

Every happy and lasting marriage has its history of many episodes of storms overcome.
Look what the Scriptures say to the married woman:

> *So he is pulled in two directions. Unmarried women and women who have never been married worry only about pleasing the Lord, and they keep their bodies and minds pure. But a married woman worries about the things of this world, because she wants to please her husband. (1 Corinthians 7:34, CEV)*

It will also give you the wisdom to then extend to your other aspirations, be it work, vocation and ministerial tasks, giving priority to decorating the marriage relationship as the number one thing in your life.

Commitment to God and dedication to your husband will be your priorities, and all selfishness will be broken from both of your lives.
Seek God together! This is powerful.

Every happy and lasting marriage has its history of many episodes of storms overcome.

21 I WOULD LIKE TO FALL IN LOVE WITH A GREAT MAN

> *"A great man sets limits on his relationship with the opposite sex, that is, with another woman who is not his wife. And because he is one with his wife, they have a great emotional and spiritual connection."*

Every woman wants to find a great man (which still exists), who is loyal, loving, and faithful. My husband is one of them, and I will tell you what the characteristics are that distinguish him.

He is always looking out for me, and that makes me reciprocate with him, considering that we spend twenty-four hours a day together and we can't be far from each other because we really are one.

Love has become more and more established between us and, therefore, our passion for each other, culminating in my admiration for him because he achieves everything he sets his mind to. He loves me and makes me feel fulfilled, thus being able to fulfill my deepest dreams and desires, and he always gives priority to the family, which gives me and our children confidence and security. With one look we already know what the other wants to say or thinks. Powerful.

I love him very much and if I had to remarry my husband I would do it a thousand times, considering that we will spend eternity together in the presence of the Father, the Son, and the Holy Spirit. I thank God for uniting us in marriage thirty-three years ago.

In other cultures, being a great man may mean having more than one woman or being a sexist tyrant, when in reality the true man is a giver. He gives his semen and has a progeny of children, he gives love and receives respect, he gives protection and forms a family that loves him until the end of his days.

> **A GREAT MAN LIVES IN HOLINESS, THAT IS, SET APART FOR GOD, WITH A CALL TO SERVICE AND FIDELITY TO HIS WIFE.**

A great man lives in holiness, that is, set apart for God, with a call to service and fidelity to his wife. He does not wear masks like a happy face when he is suffering from something or someone, but he is sincere with himself and with those around him. Therefore, you, woman, sometimes must be attentive to his vulnerability because you know him better than anyone.

A great man sets limits on his relationship with the opposite sex, that is, with another woman who is not his wife. And because he is one with his wife, they have a great emotional and spiritual connection, making biblical knowledge the incessant source of wisdom.

Let us consider the fundamental and infinite value that man has for his Creator. Although fallen, God provided him with a Savior, his only son Jesus Christ of Nazareth, out of great love for all humanity. Therefore, salvation reveals to us the greatest solution and the only way to achieve holiness, "without which no one will see the Lord." That is why this man decides to live apart from God.

A great man listens to his wife when God speaks to her. I specifically remember on two occasions where we had to make very important decisions for the future of our family, and my husband believed what I was telling him had to be done. Today, after a long time, we realize that it was the Holy Spirit who guided me to give him that advice.

> **A GREAT MAN LISTENS TO HIS WIFE WHEN GOD SPEAKS TO HER.**

Qualities of a great man

Something I read that made me laugh a lot was that no matter how many hours a man spends in a gym building muscles, if he does not have moral integrity, he will not even move a hair on a woman, because what she is looking for is not in the physique. Tremendous, right?

It is very important that he is disciplined and has control to face the vicissitudes of daily life and is someone interesting to her.

When a man has vices, whether they be drugs or alcohol, that diminishes the attractiveness and passion that she may have towards him.

The story of an alcoholic man

This couple I will tell you about met when they were very young, and giving free rein to their passion from the beginning of the relationship they had sexual relations, so at the age of fifteen she was already pregnant with her first baby. They got married and the first years of living together were beautiful until he started a job where he was very tempted to drink, so it became a addiction.

His grandfather had been an alcoholic and had died of cirrhosis, his mother the same as him. She spent the entire day drunk, and of course, it was all that this boy had experienced, which created an example in him that, by "drowning in alcohol", his personal and emotional problems would be solved. Let me tell you, his wife was an excellent woman.

When I asked her if she had wanted to separate from him, she told me, many times, and that even her children asked her to, but that his qualities when he was sober made her see that he was a good man, very good and generous. He helped everyone he could financially and with food, especially her own mother.

You can't say that he was an alcoholic because of her, no, don't believe that lie. Many men blame their wife for the fact that they indulge in alcohol. No, he does because he wants to, period. That is where his self-control comes in, which not everyone wants to exercise, because it is easier to blame the other than to assume your own actions.

It is also interesting to see how there are women who maintain a committed relationship with a man over the years, especially when there are children involved and even several years of cohabitation. Some marriages, like the one in the story I am telling you, have a good ending, because today they are still together, and thanks to their faith and her tenacity who sacrificed parties or get togethers where there could be drinks, he no longer touches a drop of alcohol. But let me tell you that in life you always must know how to set limits and discover how that man who is good can become a great man like the one in the story.

Today they both believe that it was God who predestined them and united them, and they have a beautiful family. Seeing him so transformed shows that she is a great woman, because through suffering and forgiveness a marriage can be saved.

For a great man, the first wife... is she that important?

Is it true that the first wife never stops being the most important? And the love he had for her is very strong?

I wanted to capture in this book aimed at women this very moving story of someone with whom I shared my childhood and youth.

He is a great man, and he has shown it in very extreme situations, especially with the death of his first wife, so I tell you once again that good men exist.

> *When you find the person you love and whom you want to plan your life with, you never think that you could get sick and leave*

everything half done.

I loved Hilda very much, my first wife and mother of my two children, and you know my deep admiration for how she prepared herself daily to be better in every way, professionally and as a human being.

From her I learned a deep love and respect for religion and my love for God helped me overcome that great loss. I never reneged or questioned it.

It's easy to say it, but living the day to day was the most difficult, having been left alone at the time of her death with two children, six and ten years old respectively. They were the ones who gave me the strength to give my everything. I couldn't fail them so that when they would grow up, they'd say, 'my mother died and my father disappeared'.

For me it was a total change, to stop running the company that I loved, to stop solving, to stop traveling everywhere to being available twenty-four hours a day for them and taking on tasks that I had no idea about because my wife had always handled them.

And so, I went to the first parents' meetings at school, and guided them with the experience that life itself had given me thanks to my profession and the values learned from my parents.

I also remember the words of my beloved uncle, who at her wake told me: 'Everyone you see here goes to the movies, they hang out with their friends, they live their normal lives. The only one different is you who have this task ahead of you: to get back on your

feet and raise your children forward'.
And this is where you see the human miseries, which make you feel, 'Well, now let's see if this guy who got to where he got, gets ahead'.
My dear Adriana, many times I felt very alone, but I always had the conviction to give everything for my children because it is the most beautiful thing that God gave me; I must take care of them and guide them daily.
So also, nobility obliges. I want to clarify that the only unconditional person I had was my mother. That's why today my children and I are very attentive and grateful for how she helped us.
Since Hilda's absence, in my conversations with the kids I was always clear and told them: 'If dad finds a person with whom to continue his life, I will do it because tomorrow you will be grown up and you will have your life and I want to try to return to build a family'.
And so, Patricia comes into my life, and I have no doubt that God put her on my path for many things. I am grateful to have her and that she is the person I chose to continue dreaming.
This is why I remarried. She was 40 years old, that was her dream and why not do it.
She left her activity in her hometown and came with us; She got a job at a school in the area and above all things, I value her commitment to accompanying me.
That's why I told you that for me there are

two lives, and I don't compare them because each person is different; Notice that siblings from the same parents are different! I just try to be happy and for all of us to be happy. In conclusion, I never forget everything I experienced with Hilda, my first wife, and we carry her permanently in our hearts. I never stop talking about my life experience with her.

The positive man vs. the negative man

When I think about disagreements and the image of "a great man," the difference between a positive man and a negative man comes to mind. He who is positive, everything he undertakes in life must be a success, while the negative one is the one who sees everything as impossible.

> **HE WHO IS POSITIVE, EVERYTHING HE UNDERTAKES IN LIFE MUST BE A SUCCESS.**

Although both tend to do things to achieve a dream, they both have something in common, and that is that they will always want to tell you how it went for them.

The positive one has a powerful ability to get up, while the negative one needs the woman to help him. I have also understood that if life, woman, has left you disenchanted in your last relationship, you should look for that gentleman who will make you feel like a princess in his court.

Therefore, look for a positive man.

HOW TO BECOME A CONFIDENT WOMAN 22

> *"Excellent woman: there are interiorities of your personality that are your hidden potential."*

I wrote this paragraph below in my first book, titled *Man's Greatest Frustration: Not Understanding His Wife,* which I recommend you read.

> *"Another important point to keep in mind is that women at each stage of their lives can feel fulfilled or not. In this specific case, I take the example of a woman I know, who in this time that she is alone I can observe that she feels more fulfilled than ever.*
> *This does not mean that she has not felt fulfilled as a mother and as a wife. I think what is happening is that she has now discovered her true identity, her true self.*
> *She is spiritually higher than ever, and this coincides with the fact that women do not always need to have a husband or*

have someone by their side, but rather they need to first fulfill themselves and then, in addition, be a blessing to the husband, to the children and even for those around them".[4]

I want to encourage you to start with yourself and understand that there are interiorities of your personality that are your hidden potential. Don't you think that you first need to understand yourself very well to be able to continue moving forward in all those things that are paralyzed and stopped in you?

They are those unresolved issues, those unfinished conversations, and the inability to solve the root problems, since most of your loved ones do not know the depth of your suffering, such as loneliness and shame. And what can we say about those dark thoughts that often bring fear and do not allow women to live in freedom and confidence, or even see how much strength they have within them deposited by God.

For this reason, I cannot fail to mention the "virtuous woman" of Proverbs 31, from verse 10 onwards, according to the Contemporary English Version:

A truly good wife is the most precious treasure a man can find! Her husband depends on her, and she never lets him down. She is good to him every day of her life, and with her own hands she gladly makes clothes. She is like a sailing ship that brings food from across the sea. She gets up before daylight to prepare food for her family and for her

---
[4]*Chapter 9, page 92.*

> servants. She knows how to buy land and how to plant a vineyard, and she always works hard. She knows when to buy or sell, and she stays busy until late at night. She spins her own cloth, and she helps the poor and the needy. Her family has warm clothing, and so she doesn't worry when it snows. She does her own sewing, and everything she wears is beautiful. Her husband is a well-known and respected leader in the city. She makes clothes to sell to the shop owners. She is strong and graceful, as well as cheerful about the future. Her words are sensible, and her advice is thoughtful. She takes good care of her family and is never lazy. Her children praise her, and with great pride her husband says, "There are many good women, but you are the best!" Charm can be deceiving, and beauty fades away, but a woman who honors the Lord deserves to be praised. Show her respect—praise her in public for what she has done.

"Powerful; rich; excellent; morally just; with foundation, integrity, skills and strength; powerful as an army." How many times as a woman have you avoided a potential disaster in your home?

This is a reflection that my husband wrote about wisdom and knowledge, and I thought it was very appropriate for this chapter of the book. I share it with you.

> Those who find true wisdom obtain the tools for understanding, (knowledge) the

right way to live, because they will have a fountain of blessing pouring into their lives. Obtaining the riches of wisdom is much better than obtaining all the goods in the world. (Proverbs 3:13, paraphrased)

TRUE WISDOM IS THE KEY TO LIVING PROPERLY.

This passage tells us that true wisdom is the key to living properly, but what does wisdom mean? "Set of broad and deep knowledge that is acquired through study, to act sensibly, prudently and correctly, it also enables us to reflect, draw conclusions that give us discernment of the truth, the good and the bad."

It also mentions tools for understanding, which is related to knowledge. What does understanding mean?: "Faculty of the mind that allows one to learn, understand, reason, make decisions and form a specific idea of reality, to act with good judgment, prudence, reflection, good sense and responsibility".

Broad and deep knowledge is obtained through study, effort, and personal investment. The Lord says that his people perish because they lack knowledge, they lack study, they lack effort, they lack knowing how to invest in themselves.

What God wants is for us to achieve "…the right way to live, because you will have a fountain of blessing pouring into your lives" … Excellent, right?

I always teach that we must form ourselves from our knowledge of God, since you learn to be a woman from culture, friends, or family, who are the ones who tell you that you should be this or that way. In the case of man, he is always prepared to be strong and kill his enemy.

When both reach adulthood, they do not always reach this ideal, feeling frustrated and do not value themselves, nor understand the function for which they were created.

There are women who never reach the ideal of beauty, others who join other women to enhance their nonconformity with being of the female gender, and thus spend their lives fighting to occupy a place that is not their rightful place.

Umberto Eco, in his book "History of Beauty", reveals to us, through Plotinus: "In reality there is no more authentic beauty than the wisdom that we find and appreciate in certain people. Ignoring their face, which may be unattractive, and ignoring appearance, we look for their inner beauty".[5]

This leads us to the conclusion that there is no external beauty without internal beauty as the Word of God says: *"a glad heart makes a cheerful face"* (Proverbs 15:13). There is nothing better than understanding that God thinks of you, knowing that the God who created the universe stops to think about you, and cares about you and has set his eyes on you.

> THE WOMAN WHO SUCCEEDS IS THE ONE WHO HAS A SPIRITUAL LIFE.

---

[5]*Published by Debolsillo (September 27, 2016).*

I believe a lot in inner joy and what God does within each woman, because He is the one who works from the inside out.

The woman who succeeds is the one who has a spiritual life. As you get closer to God you will understand the idiosyncrasies of that man that you cannot handle. Even if you are on different spiritual levels, the Lord will bless your marriage because you resort to prayer and intimate communion with Him. You must have an open and non-legalistic attitude. That's why the Bible says:

> *Do not be conformed to this world, but be transformed by the renewal of your mind, that by testing you may discern what is the will of God, what is good and acceptable and perfect. (Romans 12:2)*

You must have a different way of thinking. Being the same as everyone else is a deception and a very big void because you do not experience true security, trust in your relationships, both marital and with other people.
You must build your life, first, on stable ground, from tenderness, fidelity to God and generosity towards others.

You must build
your life, first, on
stable ground,
from tenderness,
fidelity to God
and generosity
towards others.

I WANT TO BE RICH   23

"Dreams are useless if they are only in your head, and you never act on them. To see your dreams fulfilled, you should not give up easily."

Both men and women can make money. That is why it is not bad that you as a woman want to be rich. By nature, we are capable of conceiving and giving life, how much more so to produce and create, because everything is about a divine gift that is within us.

It is God who gives the power to make wealth. Deuteronomy 8:18 says: "You shall remember the Lord your God, for it is he who gives you power to get wealth…"
I know that one of the virtues of a woman is to be a very good administrator and generous, because when there is abundance, she gives. Therefore, it is essential that you yourself work on your self-esteem, on your inner being to be prepared for future successes, because they will always come.

Furthermore, it is God's desire for us to "prosper in all things, in health, even as our soul prospers…" says the Bible in 3 John 2.

And for us to enjoy...

How many of you didn't celebrate a birthday? Or maybe you never went on vacation, or you never celebrated Christmas with gifts or surprises.
Well, it's time for you to do it and start with yourself. Celebrate your birthday and reschedule your life so that every year you do something new and surprising.

My husband and I schedule a trip to the mountains a month before our wedding anniversary. In addition, we choose gifts to exchange when it comes time for our romantic dinner, whether in a restaurant or in our beautiful and cozy house that we have. But above all things we do not forget to thank God for another year that we live together, enjoy family, and serve in the Ministry.

Women have been turned into a subject for discrimination, when the Word of God says that: *"There is neither Jew nor Greek, there is neither slave nor free, there is no male and female, for you are all one in Christ Jesus"* (Galatians 3:28, ESV).

This means that not only is there a social reality in the man-woman concept, but there is a much deeper and more valid biblical truth that shows us the place where God has women. Despite all social and cultural advances, the best source to recognize our identity is in the Word of God.

The ability to enjoy is within you, not outside or in people, but within you. If you are going to study like someone else did and got there, it is

> **THE ABILITY TO ENJOY IS WITHIN YOU, NOT OUTSIDE OR IN PEOPLE, BUT WITHIN YOU.**

precisely for that reason, to learn and not to envy them.

I once read this: "There are two kinds of people: those who fly and those who hang on to those who fly." Which of the two are you? Look at yourself closely, you probably have wings, and you didn't realize it. Tremendous.

Dreams are useless if they are only in your head, and you never act on them. To see your dreams fulfilled you should not give up easily. And that man who lives with you may be the one who believes in you the least, because of familiarity, because he knows your weaknesses and your character. In short, even because of jealousy, which stops your creativity, your decision-making capacity and even your way of thinking.

TO SEE YOUR DREAMS FULFILLED YOU SHOULD NOT GIVE UP EASILY.

Jealousy is normal in a relationship, but when it reaches extremes it becomes a very harmful relationship. Maybe because he thinks that by dedicating yourself to that company or job, he will lose you or no longer have your attention, which is why you should always make time for your husband and your home first and then your endeavors. Remember that a man cannot be alone without feeling bad about himself and that he also wants to be successful. So, it is always better to have his support, but when he sees that you start to have money, he will not oppose it. That's for sure.

We all have an assignment in life that we must fulfill. Think about what yours is, what your abilities are to start something and let it be the driving force, the enthusiasm that drives you to get up every day and fight for it and take care of it, because a popular saying says: "the eye of the master fattens the cattle." ", that is, no one is going to take care of that company or that business like you.

Nothing should distract you from your goal of becoming rich, famous, and influential.
Push with all your strength to achieve it, because you, beautiful woman, are an extraordinary idea of God for this time and for this hour.
The prosperity promised by God is a means to an end, not to accumulate, but to continually give. Then in all times and seasons it will be well with you.

NEVER ABANDON YOUR HOME 24

> *"Success in any relationship is always remembering that marriage is made up of imperfect beings who hurt and humiliate each other at times, but who at some point find the grace of forgiveness."*

In my first book, *Man's Greatest Frustration: Not Understanding His Wife,* I wrote in chapter 6 that "love affairs are simply that, adventures; the man always returns to a safe harbor, his wife".

This also applies to any other type of relationship that has to do with your husband, be it his mother, siblings, or friends; he will always come back to you.

I have a vivid and real example of a woman named Angie, a beautiful woman I know who told me her story of love and heartbreak with her husband, who for years was unfaithful with every woman he came across.

There came a time when Angie's heart hardened, so she made the decision to leave him, and she left her home with her children. Remember that I always teach that women need the security of knowing that she is the only one in a man's life.

Angie settled in the new city, and it went so well for her that she even had two jobs, the place had a beautiful beach and her children enjoyed the place tremendously, while her husband was left alone in the house, they had both bought.

It was obvious that loneliness had begun to take its toll on his life because the one who makes the mistakes is always the one who later feels the loneliest.
The silence in the house, the absence of someone to talk to and share at the table with, led him to seek God like never before and to serve in his church.

From having a neglected spiritual life, he became excellent in the area where he had to perform. Also considering that previously it was Angie who held family meetings to share the Word of God, now it was he who valued all that he had once wasted.

As time passed and seeing her husband changed, Angie returned to her home with her children. When I asked her the reason why she returned to him, her response was that she had returned for her home. I was surprised by what she told me. I thought she was going to tell me that it was because of the change in her husband, or because she loved him, but no, she came back because of the value that her home, her own home, had for her... of knowing that her children would grow up in the security of a house that was theirs, of their family. Then, little by little, she regained her love for him and today he has his own company, because to leave his life of adventures, he had to change his job where all the temptations were. Today, day by day, they are happier.

Today he loves and values Angie, and he became a faithful man, because as I said before, a man always returns to a safe harbor, his wife, and forgiveness can always save and restore a marriage.

> **FORGIVENESS CAN ALWAYS SAVE AND RESTORE A MARRIAGE.**

We go through a lot of suffering in life, through many deserts, but it is in that place where the Lord can really speak to the person. The human being is predictable, and that is the reason why the enemy studies, and knows in which area of the soul he can attack.

This is very deep and revealing. Satan works in the lives of some people with some ease because he has studied every step and every movement they make, and he attacks mainly in the thoughts and soul.

Our thoughts must grow in the light of the truth because this frees us from great anguish and disappointments. Remember that it is about a man, with his virtues and his shortcomings.

The advice is that limits must be set in certain situations, and success in any relationship is always remembering that marriage is made up of imperfect beings who hurt and humiliate each other at times, but who at some point find the grace of forgiveness.

marriage is made up of imperfect beings who hurt and humiliate each other at times, but who at some point find the grace of forgiveness.

THE MAN I CHOSE 25

"Precious woman: you have been called and separated by God for that man that you yourself chose."

Have you heard this phrase: "All men are equal"? Well actually, this is not so. When you relate to a man to marry you, you should know that you are joining a person who individually brings his own family, cultural and spiritual system.

I read that in our cells there is information from at least 4 generations, so we must know everything about the past of the person we chose for life. Investigating the memory of those who still live will allow us to reach the origins of both.

This is extremely interesting because when I look at my husband and he tells me about his maternal grandfather, whom he never met, but his mother told him his story, I can see how much of him he has inherited. His grandfather had a lot of money, he was a businessman, very intelligent, with a very strong Jewish influence, and that talent has been passed down from generation to generation. Not only my husband has that gift, but also our son Agustín, who from such a young age has dedicated himself to doing business and is doing very well.

In life we always go through different stages, and there are many things that we experience together. What has always worked is uniting our individualities. If I think about myself, my husband is truly the man I chose, whom I went to look for at his house and that day we became engaged. Everything I longed for in a man I found in him.

> **THE MOST IMPORTANT THING YOU MUST SEE IN THAT MAN IS THAT HE CARES ABOUT YOU.**

The most important thing you must see in that man is that he cares about you, that you know that he is interested in you, not only because of your appearance, nor because of how intelligent you are, but because you are the woman of his life. And if you are thinking of getting married, be careful when choosing a partner because that union will last a lifetime.

Some women want to find "everything" in a man, but they are expecting from the other person what they may not even be able to give themselves.

Above all, keep in mind that...

The man needs the woman

Research from Binghamton University in New York and University College London, with data from almost 5,705 people from 96 countries, showed that women receive a greater emotional and physical impact after separation, however, they tend to recover sooner than men.[6] Men move on, but perhaps never get over the breakup.

---

[6] *https://www.binghamton.edu/inside/index.php/inside/story/12326/study-women-hurt-more-by-breakups-but-recover-more-fully/*

THE MAN I CHOSE

Therefore, a woman must understand that with the man she chose, she will have good and bad days, happy nights, and sleepless nights, because those are the challenges that life has. When everything seems uncertain and confusing, and you have that man by your side with whom you will share those fleeting memories and where you will have a shoulder to cry on, you will know that you were never alone.

> *Wounds are healed, slights are forgotten, fatigue dissipates when you become stronger in the "the strength of his might" (Ephesians 6:10).*

I'm often surprised when I have a great spiritual battle, and, in fact, I have suffered many attacks on my marriage, because in those moments there is an inner force in me that is inexplicable, that is within me. It is a powerful divine source that flows from within me and makes me encourage my husband. It allows me to preach with more anointing and makes me believe in God's promises with much more faith.

The fact that you enter a place, and they stop to look at you means that there is something powerful in you, something that comes from your way of being and that makes you particularly unique. It is there that God wants you to appreciate the way He made you for that man and to feel appreciated, because that is what makes you attractive to him. If you think that you are nobody and that you have no value, that will be the treatment you will receive.

NEVER GIVE UP ON YOURSELF, YOU ARE YOUR BEST DESIGN.

Never give up on yourself, you are your best design. The mere fact that you are still alive is because you are a beautiful project of God, and his blessing enriches us and adds no sorrow. (see Proverbs 10:22).

Everything you need, look for it in God, look for the authenticity of his love, because you have been called and separated by Him for that man that you yourself chose. If you face the changes in your life based on the promises of God, you will become a wise woman and you will overcome.

His arms are outstretched, and the Lord waits for you, for that brave and determined woman who once again with a sparkle in her eyes decides to believe that it is possible to change and try again.

Wounds are healed, slights are forgotten, fatigue dissipates when you become stronger in the "the strength of his might"

EPILOGUE
From my heart

To write this second book "Woman's greatest frustration: not understanding her husband", I want to tell you that I emptied myself of guilt, anger, nerves, sentimental dependence, charges of conscience, bad thoughts, words that caused me harm and so many other things.

Why do I want to capture this? Because I know that whoever reads this book will be helped, and because to live well one must be strong in the Lord and in the strength of His Might (see Ephesians 6:10)

Let's speak words of health, of healing, of victory...let's pay more attention to all the factors that surround us, because we are so difficult sometimes to recognize the gifts in others...right?

But turning your heart to God and turning inward to continue giving encouragement to your husband, your children, your parents, in short, will require vigilance on your part, yes, vigilance so that they do not harm you.

Do not live in a "false freedom", holding a shame that does not belong to you. You are destined to be a blessing wherever you are.

I once read that a former first lady of the United States was asked, "What would you have done if you had married your high school sweetheart, who became a moderately prosperous farmer? You would not have had the opportunity to become first lady." She replied: "Oh, of course I would have made it. That old farmer would have become the president of the United States." The truth is that this life is for the hardworking and those who are not afraid of anything.

Lastly, when you go through so many difficult situations, what will keep you strong is your faith. Never lose faith and you must always grow, never stop, because we are here to be a blessing and to let the promises of the Lord flow forth.

I wish that spiritual, mental, and physical strength comes upon you to move forward. Don't stop, woman, God is with you. I bless you from my heart.

FINAL WORDS

Thank you for allowing me to provide you with a little more wisdom so that you understand your purpose and your assignment. From now on, it is my wish that you can make the most important changes in your life, which must be lasting and eternal.

I cannot conclude without introducing you to Jesus Christ as your personal Savior. Wherever you are, say this prayer:

> *Lord Jesus Christ, I ask your forgiveness for all my sins. I confess you as my only and sufficient Savior. I declare with my mouth that Jesus Christ has come in the flesh, for the glory of God. Holy Spirit, fill my life, and help me to pray. In the name of Jesus Christ. Amen.*

May God bless you and keep you, and make his face shine upon you, and give you peace. Shalom.

> *For God so loved the world, that he gave his only Son, that whoever believes in him should not perish but have eternal life. (John 3:16, ESV).*

ABOUT THE AUTHOR

Dr. Adriana Calabria is an international speaker for women and couples, doctoral minister in Theology and Pastoral Care. Communicator par excellence and counselor with extensive empathy in interpersonal relationships, she writes books with very inspiring and original titles. The first is Man's Greatest Frustration: Not Understanding His Wife, which in a very short time had great success.

With this second book in the saga, Woman's Greatest Frustration: Not Understanding Her Husband, comes to bring us with its charisma and sympathy a gift for the soul of the woman who wants to get out of the routine and build healthy relationships, mainly with her husband.

She has the heart of a writer with a passion that motivates everyone who reads her books.
Many pastors use them as a teaching manual in their churches.
She has received numerous testimonies where in certain chapters some cried, and others laughed because they felt moved by its content.
Her writings achieve a more egalitarian concept of men and women, always respecting the divine order.

Dr. Adriana Calabria with her husband Apostle Osvaldo Díaz have a marriage of 33 years, 3 children, Agustín married to Saraí originally from Mexico who have two boys Ethan and Liam, Damaris married to an Italian Domenico, and they have a girl Arianna, and the third daughter is Daniela who studies at the North Carolina University of Charlotte.

They all reside in the state of North Carolina and serve God together with Apostles Osvaldo and Adriana in the International Celebración Osvaldo Diaz Ministries, with headquarters in different countries.

Adriana Calabria

For presentations, conferences, preaching and book sales, please contact

Damaris Diaz
919-229-6650

adrianacalabria.com

www.ingramcontent.com/pod-product-compliance
Lightning Source LLC
Chambersburg PA
CBHW050906160426
43194CB00011B/2304